Peter Lawrence's Fellow Travellers offers insights I have not found else-where, a fascinating exploration of the experience of followers of Jesus from three neighbouring but distinct religious communities in the Holy Land. Lawrence adds significantly to our understanding of 'in Messiah' identity and identity formation in communitarian cultures, an innovative and welcome study.

David Greenlee, editor of *Longing for Community: Church,* Ummah, *or Somewhere in Between?*

This ground-breaking comparative study of Messianic Jews, Arab Evangelicals and Muslim-Background Believers in the Holy Land not only compares and contrasts the experiences of faith and identity formation amongst these groups, but also provides a wealth of materials, resources and insights for anyone wishing to understand and engage in ministry in this challenging context. Peter Lawrence's work brings cutting edge research of the highest standard to the field and is strongly recommended.

Richard Harvey, author of *Mapping Messianic Jewish Theology*

In this important work Lawrence provides us with a fascinating comparative study of identity formation among Jesus Followers in the Holy Land, reminding us of the multi-layered complexity of Messiah-centred faith lived out in Israel today.

Duane Alexander Miller, author of *Arab Evangelicals in Israel* and *Living among the Breakage*

This study is unique because it compares groups of Jesus Followers that have such a different cultural and religious background, even while they live in the same geographical and political context. As I have observed the author conducting his research, I have been impressed by the precision of his questioning, the empathy with the people concerned, and the understanding of the complicated issue of religious and social identity. In analysing the outcomes of his enquiry, he has created bridges, enriched our understanding and opened new perspectives.

Evert Van de Poll, author of *Sacred Times For Chosen People*

Peter Lawrence has critically assessed various methodological approaches to suitably compare the identity formation of Messianic Jews, Arab Evangelicals and Muslim-Background Believers in the Holy Land. He demonstrates an impressive familiarity with the literature in his field of research, even uncovering hidden theses and marginal publications. Lawrence has raised so many open questions, that I would very much like to see him pursue the doctorate which he humbly wanted to leave to others! Congratulations!

Christof Sauer, editor of *Bad Urach Statement*

Peter Lawrence

Fellow Travellers

World of Theology Series

Published by the Theological Commission of the World Evangelical Alliance

Volume 15

Peter Lawrence

Fellow Travellers

A Comparative Study on the Identity Formation of Jesus Followers from Jewish, Christian and Muslim Backgrounds in The Holy Land

WIPF & STOCK · Eugene, Oregon

Wipf and Stock Publishers
199 W 8th Ave, Suite 3
Eugene, OR 97401

Fellow Travellers
A Comparative Study on the Identity Formation of Jesus
Followers from Jewish, Christian and Muslim Backgrounds
in The Holy Land
By Lawrence, Peter
Copyright © 2020 Verlag für Kultur und Wissenschaft
Culture and Science Publ. All rights reserved.
Softcover ISBN-13: 978-1-7252-8969-7
Publication date 10/23/2020
Previously published by Verlag für Kultur und Wissenschaft
Culture and Science Publ., 2020

Contents

Abstract

Since the eighteenth century, communities of evangelical faith have emerged in the Holy Land. The personal and collective experiences of their members have been researched but, thus far, never compared. This research project is a first attempt to conduct a comparative study on these Jesus followers with a particular focus on the formation of their core, social and corporate identities.

Based on this objective, the central research question of this thesis is stated as follows: "How can the identity formation of Messianic Jews, Arab Evangelicals and Muslim-background believers in Israel be described and in what way are their personal and collective experiences similar and/or dissimilar in this domain?"

From the data collected through a literature review and the data generated from a field study – i.e. nine semi-structured interviews with members of the target groups in the north of Israel – the terminology of 'being on a journey' has emerged to describe the identity formation of these Jesus followers. This thesis will demonstrate that although they might have the same destination in mind, at times, they take different routes. Nevertheless, when they encounter each other on their faith journey – as fellow travellers – there is a strong sense of connection and belonging between these believers of evangelical faith.

This thesis makes a valuable contribution to the field of missiology by presenting a missiological framework for a comparative study between Messianic Jews, Arab Evangelicals and Muslim-background believers in Israel. The author will contend that the presence of these communities of evangelical faith in a small geographical area provides a unique opportunity for research on missiological topics – such as 'Insider Movements' – which are of great interest for scholars and practitioners in this field of study.

Acknowledgements

This thesis could not have been completed without the support of the following people and institutions.

I would like to thank my advisor Prof Dr Evert van de Poll for his continuous feedback and encouragement throughout this research project. I feel honoured to have worked with such an esteemed scholar. Furthermore, I want to express my gratitude towards all my professors and fellow students at the ETF. By asking questions, they have demonstrated their interest in my research project and given me meaningful insights throughout the process.

Over the last three years, I have received a scholarship from my home congregation in the Netherlands. I will feel forever grateful for the financial and prayer support they have given me throughout this time and beyond.

My field study could not have been conducted without the assistance of my gatekeepers. I want to thank them for giving me access to nine believers of evangelical faith in the north of Israel. I also want to express my gratitude towards the interviewees for sharing their life stories with me. Their faith journey has been a great inspiration for my own walk with the Lord. I hope that one day I will meet them again in the Holy Land.

The moral support of my friends and family members has been instrumental in completing this thesis. I want to thank them for their acts of love, kindness and generosity. Especially Rebecca, my wife, has been my greatest encourager and supporter throughout this process. I want to thank her for listening to me at supper after a long day in the office.

In conclusion, I want to give God all the glory for strengthening and equipping me throughout this research project. I pray that the findings of the thesis will be used for establishing his kingdom on this earth.

Table of Figures

1: Introduction

On a car journey from Jerusalem to the Sea of Galilea, the long-awaited question was asked by a close friend: "Should Muslim women continue to wear a veil after they have come to faith in Jesus?" The answer provided might have been shallow but, in that moment, a desire was born to find a thorough response to that question. In the years that followed, countless books were read and numerous papers written on this topic by the author of this thesis. And, each time, a new layer behind the original question was uncovered. This research project is the final product of an inquiry that was ignited by a simple remark from a dear friend.

Through the personal encounter with Jesus followers from a Jewish, Muslim and Christian background in the Middle East, over a period of twelve years, the author of this thesis started to wonder if the question posed by his friend might be pointing towards a more profound issue faced by members of these target groups. Namely, how do they (re-) negotiate their identity in relation to their religion of birth and their newly-found faith? Which elements do they (want to) hold on to and which do they leave behind? How do they form their identity and practice their faith in the community in which they were born and raised? And, do they make the same or similar choices in this process? The accumulation of these questions resulted in a research proposal for a master's thesis in the field of religious studies and missiology at the Evangelical Theological Faculty in Leuven, Belgium.[1]

This introductory chapter will provide a brief background to the inquiry, present the purpose and anticipated contribution of the research project, formulate the central research question and sub-questions, suggest a research design and provide an insight into the researcher's background.

---

[1] In spring 2020 this research project was completed and a thesis with the title "Fellow Travellers; A Comparative Study on the Identity Formation of Messianic Jews, Arab Evangelicals and Muslim-Background Believers in Israel" was submitted in partial fulfilment of the requirements for a degree of Master of Arts in Theology and Religious Studies. The advisor for this research project was Prof Dr Evert van de Poll and the external readers were Dr Richard Harvey and Prof Dr Christof Sauer. The master's thesis was passed with high honours (17/20) in July 2020.

1.1   Background

From the eighteenth century onwards, communities of evangelical faith
have emerged in the Middle East. Due to the influence of foreign mission
workers, locals left their religion of birth and joined evangelical Protestantism. Although the initial response was slow, the number of believers
of evangelical faith has increased rapidly over the last decades. Especially
among members of the House of Islam, many have come to faith in Christ.
There is also a growing number of Jews who have accepted Jesus as their
Messiah. Although Christians from the Orthodox and Catholic churches
were the first to respond to the gospel call of Protestant mission workers,
their number has decreased significantly in recent decades because many
of them have immigrated to the West. However, if combined, members of
these communities of evangelical faith – namely; Messianic Jews, Arab
Evangelicals and Muslim-background believers – have a significant presence in the Holy Land.

 The growth of believers with evangelical faith in Israel and the wider
region has not stayed unnoticed in the academic world. The personal and
collective experiences of these Jesus followers have been researched by
scholars from the fields of sociology, anthropology, psychology, pedagogy,
theology and missiology. Most of these studies provide a fresh and unique
insight into the faith practices and religious beliefs of these Jesus followers. And, even though scholars often refer to and make use of the findings
from other fields of study – as will be demonstrated in the literature review
– they approach the topic from their own field of expertise. Subsequently,
the experiences of Jesus followers are explored from the angle of culture,
history, religion, education or social structures. This is an important consideration, because the field of study to which these scholars belong
guides, to a large extent, the questions that they are raising. This thesis
will study the identity formation of Messianic Jews, Arab Evangelicals and
Muslims-background believers from a missiological perspective.

1.2   Purpose and Anticipated Contribution

In recent decades, extensive research has been conducted by missiologists among believers of evangelical faith in the Middle East. Their focus
has been mainly on the topics of evangelism, conversion, discipleship and
church planting. Notably, the issue of contextualisation – related to each
of these four subjects – has especially drawn much interest and, subsequently, controversy in the missiological community of scholars and

practitioners.[2] From these discussions, the topic of identity formation has emerged as a research gap within the field of missiology.[3] Consequently, popular books and academic articles have been published on this particular issue, most notably about Muslim-background believers in the Middle East, Asia and Africa. Limited research, however, has been done among believers of evangelical faith in Israel. Hence, the aim of this thesis is, first of all, to bring together the available data through a literature review and generate new data by conducting semi-structured interviews with members of the target groups.[4] Secondly, thus far, no comparative study has been done on believers of evangelical faith in the Holy Land. This research project will be a first attempt to compare their experiences – with a particular focus on identity formation – of Messianic Jews, Arab Evangelicals and Muslim-background believers in the north of Israel.[5] For these reasons, this thesis will provide a unique contribution to the field of missiology.

1.3   Central Research Question & Sub-Questions

In order to meet the objectives stated above, the central research question of this thesis is as follows:

> How can the identity formation of Messianic Jews, Arab Evangelicals and Muslim-background believers in Israel be described and in what way are their personal and collective experiences similar and/or dissimilar in this domain?

---

[2]   Contextualisation is generally understood as the study on the relationship between faith and culture in a mission context. Miller provides an in-depth overview of some of the main issues at play – with regards to this topic – within the field of missiology. Duane Alexander Miller, *Living among the Breakage: Contextual Theology-Making and Ex-Muslim Christians* (Eugene, Oregon: Pickwick Publications, 2016), 13–23.

[3]   Greenlee, for example, noticed this change in research objectives between the first and second 'Coming to Faith Consultation' which were held in 2004 and 2010. David Greenlee, ed., *Longing for Community: Church, Ummah, or Somewhere in Between?* (Pasadena, CA: William Carey Library, 2013), XIV.

[4]   Due to the vast amount of research done in this field of study. the aim of the literature review is to cover – first and foremost – the breadth rather than the depth of the data available.

[5]   The reasons for limiting the geographical area of the research project to the State of Israel will be explained in §6.2.

The central research question will be answered by addressing the following sub-questions:

1. In what way do members of the target groups encounter levels of *continuity* and/or *discontinuity* in their core, social and corporate identities with regards to their cultural and religious backgrounds?
2. In what way do members of the target groups pursue a *new* and/or *renewed* identity as Jesus followers?
3. In what way do members of the target groups form their identity in a *similar* and/or *dissimilar* way?

1.4   Research Design

The central research question and sub-questions will be answered through a literature review and a field study. In chapter 2, a historical overview will be provided of the three communities of evangelical faith in the Holy Land. Following on from this, the points of commonality between members of these target groups will be discussed in chapter 3 and, subsequently, a strong case will be made to justify a comparative study. In chapter 4, an overview will be provided of the main findings from academic research and field studies on the identity formation of Messianic Jews, Arab Evangelicals and Muslim-Background believers. From the vast amount of data collected, a limited number of concepts and themes will be selected in chapter 5 in order to build a missiological framework for a comparative study. Chapter 6 will describe the process of conducting semi-structured interviews in the north of Israel and outline the research methodology used in this field study. The findings will be presented in chapter 7 and, subsequently, discussed in chapter 8. Furthermore, the central research question and sub-questions will be answered based on the data collected from the literature review and generated through the field study. In addition, the possible implications for the field of missiology will be explored and recommendations for further research will be made. Chapter 9 will provide an overview of the processes, findings, achievements and contributions of the research project. Furthermore, the author will reflect on the outcomes of his thesis.

1.5   Terminology

Thus far, the terminology used in this thesis has been as clear and straightforward as possible. However, the author is keenly aware of the sensitivities surrounding a number of these social, religious, political, historical and geographical terms.[6] However, it is impossible to conduct this research project without referring to the terminology commonly-used in academic literature. For this reason, readers are advised to take a neutral stance towards some of these loaded terms as the author tries to navigate carefully through these sensitive matters.

In chapter 2 and 3, the terminology used in this thesis will be explained and, where necessary, a definition will be provided. However, there are a number of terms that need to be clarified in this introductory chapter.

Firstly, Messianic Jews, Arab Evangelical and Muslim-background believers in Israel are commonly referred to as 'believers', 'Jesus followers', 'members of the target group' or 'believers of evangelical faith'. Furthermore, the following abbreviations will be used to refer to members of each group: MJs, AEs and MBBs. The order in which these groups are discussed is based on the number of people belonging to these communities of evangelical faith in Israel.

Secondly, the term 'conversion' is used carefully in this thesis due to the great sensitivity around this word among members of the target groups; especially among Messianic Jews. However, if applied by the author, it refers generally to the socio-religious understanding of this term – i.e. 'change of faith and/or religious affiliation'. Based on this broad and common definition, Rambo lists five types of conversion – namely: *institutional transition, affiliation, intensification, apostasy* and *defection* – which demonstrates that the meaning of the word is multi-layered and, therefore, should be used carefully.[7] Within the field of missiology, there is much debate on the biblical definition of the term 'conversion'. Barnett suggests, for example, that it merely refers to "turning towards God".[8] From his understanding of the Scriptures, he argues that 'Christian conversion' is more concerned about the *internal process* – namely, a commitment to Jesus as Lord – than the *external process* – i.e. whether a new believer has to leave his or her community and/or religion of birth in order

---

[6]   This issue is widely acknowledged in the literature and a similar approach – as presented in this section – has been suggested by the following scholars: Greenlee, *Longing for Community*, 235.; Craig A Dunning, 'Palestinian Muslims Converting to Christianity: Effective Evangelistic Methods in the West Bank.' (Pretoria, University of Pretoria, 2013), 5–7.

[7]   Lewis R. Rambo, *Understanding Religious Conversion* (New Haven: Yale University Press, 1993), 38–39.

[8]   Other terms used for this specific understanding of conversion are: 'born-again', 'saved', 'coming to faith', and so forth. Jens Barnett, 'Conversion's Consequences: Identity, Belonging, and Hybridity amongst Muslim Followers of Christ [Unpublished Thesis]' (Redcliffe College, 2008), 33–34.

to follow Jesus. Although Barnett's argument is not without merit, it is impossible to apply this particular definition of 'conversion' throughout a comparative study. The aim of this research project is *to explore* rather than *to discuss* and to be *descriptive* rather than *normative*. Therefore, the term 'conversion' could cover a wide spectrum of meanings – ranging from 'change of faith and/or religious affiliation' to 'turning towards God' – in this thesis depending on the scholar or interviewee cited.[9] However, the author will ensure that the reader understands the definition referred to and will be consistent in his own use of this word as defined above.

Thirdly, the term 'evangelical' is not easily defined, either as a *noun* or an *adjective*. Most scholars provide a historical overview of Evangelicalism rather than a definition of this word. Larsen, however, attempts to define it as follows:

> An evangelical is: 1. an orthodox Protestant; 2. who stands in the tradition of the global Christian networks arising from the eighteenth-century revival movements associated with John Wesley and George Whitefield; 3. who has a preeminent place for the Bible in her or his Christian life as the divinely inspired, final authority in matters of faith and practice; 4. who stresses reconciliation with God through the atoning work of Jesus Christ on the cross; 5. and who stresses the work of the Holy Spirit in the life of an individual to bring about conversion and an ongoing life of fellowship with God and service to God and others, including the duty of all believers to participate in the task of proclaiming the gospel to all people.[10]

Although this definition is helpful, it is impossible to use such a detailed description of a label in a comparative study. Furthermore, Van de Poll points out that the word merely refers to the "good news of Jesus Christ".[11] From a historical perspective, the name has been associated with Protestantism in Europe and, later on, with the Pietistic and revivalist movements within this church denomination around the world. Nowadays, he suggests, the term refers to "a number of 'Evangelical' or 'Free church' denominations, ranging from Baptists to Pentecostals" and more broadly to

---

[9]   A similar approach is taken, for example, by Greenlee as editor of an influential book on the identity formation of Muslim-background believers. Greenlee, *Longing for Community*, XVIII.

[10]   Timothy Larsen and Daniel J. Treier, eds., *The Cambridge Companion to Evangelical Theology*, Cambridge Companions to Religion (Cambridge New York: Cambridge University Press, 2007), 1.

[11]   Evert Van de Poll, *Sacred Times for Chosen People: Development, Analysis and Missiological Significance of Messianic Jewish Holiday Practice*, Mission, no. 46 (Zoetermeer: Boekencentrum, 2008), 28.

"the Charismatic movements in the historical churches (Protestant, Roman Catholic, Orthodox)… inasmuch as they share its spirituality, its emphasis on personal faith and its adherence to the authority of the Scriptures."[12] Based on these criteria suggested by Van de Poll, the target groups are called 'communities of evangelical faith' in this thesis. The reasons for not using the label 'evangelical' to refer to Messianic Jews and Muslim-background believers but 'believers of evangelical faith' will be explained in §3.5.

Fourthly, the term 'Holy Land' refers to the geographical area between the Jordan river and the Mediterranean Sea, both *past* and *present*.[13] However, the main focus of this research project is on the identity formation of members of the target groups residing in the State of Israel – as mentioned before – and, therefore, the term 'Israel' is most commonly used in this thesis. Occasionally, the author refers to the 'West Bank' in order to clarify that he refers to the people and/or cities of the Palestinian territories.

In the literature review, it will become evident that the terms mentioned above are highly contested and fiercely debated within the field of missiology and religious studies. Also, the interviewees struggled greatly to find the right words to express their views and describe their experiences. Although it is impossible to do everyone justice, as terms carry different meanings for those involved in the discussion, the author will be considerate of the sensitivities around the terminology and – at the same time – be consistent in using the definitions, as listed above, throughout this thesis.

---

12 Although members of Evangelical churches might be called 'evangelicals', it should be pointed out that they might not all meet the criteria suggested by Van de Poll. Therefore, it is possible to have 'non-evangelical' members in these Evangelical churches. Furthermore, the non-evangelical members of the traditional churches are often referred to as 'nominal Christians' in the literature and by the interviewees and, as such, this label will be used in this thesis. However, the author is aware of the discussion around this term – as demonstrated, for example, in the 'The Lausanne Rome 2018 Statement on Nominal Christianity' – but is not going to engage in this debate in this thesis. Van de Poll, 28–29.; Lausanne Global Consulation, 'The Lausanne Rome 2018 Statement on Nominal Christianity [Accessed 10/11/2019]' (Lausanne Global Consultation on Nominal Christianity, Rome, 2018), https://www.lausanne.org/content/statement/missing-christians-global-call.

13 Ant Greenham, 'Muslim Conversions to Christ: An Investigation of Palestinian Converts Living in the Holy Land' (Wake Forest, NC, Southeastern Baptist Theological Seminary, 2004), 15.

1.6   Researcher's Background

Since 2006, the researcher has been closely connected to believers of evangelical faith in the Holy Land and, more generally, to the peoples of the Middle East. Through his three years of ministry with a Messianic congregation in the north of Israel and three years of service with a Christian educational institution in the West Bank, he has formed close friendships with former colleagues, students, roommates, neighbours and church members. This network of friends and acquaintances proved to be invaluable during his field study as will be become clear in chapter 6. Furthermore, the researcher has participated frequently in congregational meetings and holiday practices with members of the target groups for more than twelve years. This has given him an insight into the religious experiences of these Jesus followers in the Holy Land. Also, his exposure to Israeli society, with all its ethnic and religious diversity, has been a source of great insight into the complexity of the region. And, finally, his ability to converse in Hebrew and, to a lesser extent, Arabic has given him access to literature and members of the target groups that would otherwise remain out of reach of the academic world. All of these connections, experiences, insights and competencies will have a profound effect on the researcher's ability to answer the central research question and sub-questions – although it is not without difficulties, as will be discussed in §6.2 and §9.3.

On a car journey through the Jordan valley, a close friend asked the author a question which led to the inquiry of this thesis. Four years later, they have returned to northern Israel – but this time as husband and wife – for a life of long-term ministry among the peoples they are called to serve in the Middle East. This thesis is dedicated to and seeks to benefit those who follow Jesus in the Holy Land.

2: Communities of Evangelical Faith in the Holy Land

The revival movement that swept through Britain and North American in the eighteenth and nineteenth century, also reached the Holy Land. This chapter will provide a brief overview of the birth and growth of three communities of evangelical faith in the land where the gospel was first preached.[14]

2.1 Messianic Jews

The first record of Jesus-believing Jews can be found in the New Testament. Twelve men of Jewish descent were called by Jesus to follow him and become fishers of men.[15] As they walked with him through the land of Israel, they saw the miracles he performed and heard the words of eternal life that he spoke. When asked directly by Jesus "who do you say that I am?", Peter could only respond by saying "You are the Christ, the Son of the living God."[16] Although their faith was severely tested by the arrest and crucifixion of their rabbi, his resurrection became a source of hope for this community of Jesus followers. Through the empowerment of the Holy Spirit, they were sent out from Jerusalem to the ends of the earth as heralds of the good news.

The members of the Early Church were, by and large, believers from Jewish descent – including those who had converted to Judaism – and resided in either Palestine or the diaspora. Although they are often called the first Christians, from their point of view, they had not converted from Judaism to another religion but rather experienced a 'conversion' within their own community of birth.[17] They saw themselves as a sect within Second Temple Judaism – also, called the 'Nazarenes' or 'followers of the way'

---

[14]   It should be pointed out, that there are other communities of evangelical faith in the State of Israel – i.e. migrant and international churches – but these cannot be considered indigenous. Furthermore, as pointed out in §1.5, the author acknowledges as well that there are believers of evangelical faith in traditional churches.

[15]   Mark 1:17

[16]   Matthew 16:15-16. All references from Scripture are taken for the English Standard Version unless indicated otherwise.

[17]   Jacobus (Kobus) Kok and John Anthony Dunne, eds., *Insiders versus Outsiders: Exploring the Dynamic Relationship between Mission and Ethos in the New Testament*, Perspectives on Philosophy and Religious Thought 14 (Piscataway: Gorgias Press, 2014), 2.

– and worshipped with their kinsman in the synagogues as Jews who had found their Messiah.[18] Only in the second century – as a result of the parting(s) of the ways – Jewish believers in Jesus were gradually forced to choose between either Rabbinic Judaism or Hellenistic Christianity, because they had become an ethnic minority in the increasingly 'gentilised' Church. With the conversion of Constantine and the Christianisation of the Roman empire in the fourth century, the separation was complete. The Church no longer allowed believers of Jewish decent to observe and practice any form of Judaism. Cohn-Sherbok points out that they even had to denounce their own people and heritage in order to demonstrate their commitment to Christendom.[19] Consequently, Jesus-believing Jews that remained in the Church became – by and large – invisible members until the eighteenth century.

Due the rise of 'restorationist eschatology' within Protestantism, first by the Puritans and later on by the Evangelicals, there arose a renewed interest in the Jewish members of the Church – according to Van de Poll.[20] Based on their understanding of Scripture, they foresaw a return of the Jewish people to their Messiah and their homeland.[21] Both events would precede and inaugurate the imminent return of Christ.[22] Motivated by this eschatological understanding, mission agencies were formed and hundreds of Protestant mission workers were sent out to share the gospel with Jews in North America, Europe and Palestine. By the end of the nineteenth century more than 200,000 Jews had been baptised.[23] Most of these new

---

[18] Dan Cohn-Sherbok, *Messianic Judaism* (London ; New York: Continuum, 2000), 3–4. A more detailed account of this movement can be found in: Ray A. Pritz, *Nazarene Jewish Christianity: From the End of the New Testament Period until Its Disappearance in the Fourth Century* (Jerusalem: Magnes Press, 1992).

[19] Cohn-Sherbok, *Messianic Judaism*, 6.

[20] Van de Poll, *Sacred Times for Chosen People*, 40–45.

[21] Kai Kjaer-Hansen, ed., *Jewish Identity and Faith in Jesus* (Jerusalem: Caspari Center, 1996), 97.

[22] It should be pointed out that, during the nineteenth century, Protestant mission was strongly influenced by various forms of millennialism. The second coming of Christ was a strong motivator for commissioning mission workers to the far corners of the earth. David Jacobus Bosch, *Transforming Mission: Paradigm Shifts in Theology of Mission*, American Society of Missiology Series, no. 16 (Maryknoll, N.Y: Orbis Books, 1991), 313–27.

[23] Van de Poll suggests that these figures should be taken with considerable caution as they are largely based on reports from mission agencies. Richard Harvey, however, pointed out in his correspondence with the author of this thesis that De La Roi's baptism statistics can be considered reliable. Van de Poll, *Sacred Times for Chosen People*, 50–51.; J. F. A. De Le Roi, *Evangelische Christenheit und die Juden* (Hansebooks, 2017).

converts – also called Hebrew Christians – became evangelical in their faith and protestant in their affiliation.

During the 'Jesus movement' that swept through North America in the 1960s and 1970s, tens of thousands of Jews came to faith in their Messiah. This time around, many of them did not join mainline Protestant or Evangelical churches but formed Messianic congregations in which they could express their newly-found faith in accordance with their Jewish heritage. By the turn of the millennium, according to some estimates, more than 300,000 people around the world identified themselves as Messianic Jews.[24]

The creation of the State of Israel and the reunification of Jerusalem had a profound effect on this generation of Jesus-believing Jews, because they viewed these events as a fulfilment of biblical prophecy.[25] Subsequently, a significant number of them immigrated to the land of their ancestors in order to be part of the regathering of the people of Israel. As a result, the number of Messianic congregations in Israel grew from 1 to 81 and the number of Messianic Jews from a few dozen to 5,000 during the second half of the twentieth century.[26] Since the turn of the millennium, there has been an exponential growth of Jesus-believing Jews in Israel. Many of them were born and raised in the Holy Land. Most recent research shows that there are around 300 Messianic congregations and 30,000 Messianic Jews in Israel.[27] The gospel movement that started with a rabbi from the Galilee became the largest religion in the world, but eventually returned to the people and land of origin.

2.2   Arab Evangelicals

Throughout history, there has always been a Christian presence in the Middle East. From the day of Pentecost, the Church established itself in the region. The apostle to the gentiles, Paul of Tarsus, travelled to "Arabia" and the "regions of Syria" to spread the good news of Jesus.[28] In the book of Acts, a group of non-Jewish disciples in the city of Antioch were called,

---

[24]   A detailed overview and discussion on the sources of these estimates can be found here: Van de Poll, *Sacred Times for Chosen People*, 100–103.

[25]   Cohn-Sherbok, *Messianic Judaism*, 63–64.

[26]   Erez Soref, 'The Messianic Jewish Movement in Modern Israel', in *Israel, the Church, and the Middle East: A Biblical Response to the Current Conflict.*, ed. Darrell L Bock and Mitch Glaser (Kregel Publications, 2018), 138–41.

[27]   Soref, 141–43.

[28]   Galatians 1:17, 20

for the first time, 'Christians'.[29] By the third century, there were numerous communities of Arab Christians throughout the Near East.[30] Denominations were formed and doctrines formulated as a result of the church councils in Nicaea and Chalcedon. With the rise of Islam, Arab Christianity became a minority religion in the Middle East. Although Christians were treated as second-class citizens, most notably under the millet system of the Ottoman empire, the Eastern churches remained present in the region. By the turn of the nineteenth century, twenty percent of the population in the Middle East was Christian.[31] They contributed greatly to society in the areas of education, health care and political reform.[32] Today, there are four families of churches in the Middle East – namely, Eastern Orthodox, Oriental Orthodox, Catholic and Protestant – who continue to be a Christian presence in the region.[33]

David Thomas points out that the term 'Arab Christianity' is, in some ways, ambiguous because the word 'Arab' refers to both a language and an ethnicity. However, Christians in the Middle East often use another language in their church services and belong to various ethnic groups. But, because of the Islamic rule in the region over the last thirteen centuries, 'Arabness' has become their main identity in daily life and, therefore, they are called Arab Christians.[34]

The city of Jerusalem has been a place of great significance for Christians throughout Church history.[35] Clergy and laity have travelled as pilgrims to the Holy Land. Similarly, foreign emperors came to Jerusalem to establish their earthly kingdom and to build their own churches. Looking back on the history of the Church, Bailey and Bailey suggest that "all spiritual roads seemed to lead to Jerusalem rather than Rome".[36] By the time

---

[29] Interestingly, Stern notes – with regards to this verse in Acts 11:26 – that the term Christian is in the New Testament only used to refer to non-Jewish believers in Christ. Further research is required to establish if this is indeed the case. David H Stern, *Messianic Jewish Manifesto* (Clarksville, MD: Jewish New Testament Publications, 1997), 30–34.

[30] David Thomas, 'Arab Christianity', in *The Blackwell Companion to Eastern Christianity*, ed. Kenneth Parry, Blackwell Companions to Religion (Malden, MA: Wiley-Blackwell, 2010), 2.

[31] Thomas, 20.

[32] Azar Ajaj, Duane Alexander Miller, and Philip Sumpter, *Arab Evangelicals in Israel* (Eugene, Oregon: Pickwick Publications, 2016), 18.

[33] Betty Jane Bailey and J. Martin Bailey, *Who Are the Christians in the Middle East?* (Grand Rapids, Mich: W.B. Eerdmans, 2003), 47.

[34] Thomas, 'Arab Christianity', 1.

[35] Bailey and Bailey, *Who Are the Christians in the Middle East?*, 32.

[36] Bailey and Bailey, 33.

of the crusades, most of the church denominations – which are currently present in Israel – were already established in the Holy Land.[37] With their religious practice came, more often than not, the political influence of their home countries. The subsequent conquests of Islamic rulers made Christians and Jews second-class citizens and they suffered greatly under their regimes. This is not to say that Christian emperors treated the local people much better during their periods of reign over Jerusalem. Because of the oppression experienced by foreign invaders throughout history, some Palestinian theologians "choose to identify themselves as the descendants of the original indigenous church".[38] While the evidence provided for this historical claim is limited, the sentiment behind this notion is understandable. Overall, the city of Jerusalem has had a great effect on the formation of Arab Christianity in the Holy Land.

The roots of Arab Evangelicalism can be traced back to the churches started by Protestant mission workers in the eighteenth and nineteenth century. Initially, they came to share the gospel with Muslims and Jews but – because of their limited success – they turned their efforts towards members of the Eastern Orthodox, Oriental Orthodox and Catholic churches.[39] This caused great friction and tension with the local clergy which can be still felt today.[40] Because of their personal dedication to the gospel (*injil*), Protestant mission workers and their first followers were called 'evangelical' (*injilleyyeh*) in Arabic.[41] Hence, this term is used synonymously with 'protestant' although there are some subtle differences. The Anglican Church is, for example, the *only* denomination recognised by the State of Israel as Protestant although some members rather identify themselves as evangelical. The other Protestant denominations in the Holy Land are represented by the Convention of Evangelical Churches in Israel (CICE) because of their commitment to "evangelical faith".[42] As such, they are trying to gain official recognition by the Israeli government as Arab Evangelicals.

---

[37] Such as: Greek Orthodox, Syrian Jacobites, Maronites, Ethiopians, Copts, Armenians, Nestorians and Georgians. Ajaj, Miller, and Sumpter, *Arab Evangelicals in Israel*, 3.

[38] Ajaj, Miller, and Sumpter, 3.

[39] Bailey and Bailey, *Who Are the Christians in the Middle East?*, 50.

[40] Kenneth Cragg, *The Arab Christian: A History in the Middle East*, 1st ed (Louisville, Ky: Westminster/John Knox Press, 1991), 135.

[41] Bailey and Bailey, *Who Are the Christians in the Middle East?*, 50.

[42] The CICE represents five ecclesial families in Israel, namely the Baptists, Assemblies of God, Open Brethren, Church of the Nazarene and Christian Missionary Alliance. Ajaj, Miller, and Sumpter, *Arab Evangelicals in Israel*, 34–36.

There are approximately 5,000 Arab Evangelicals in Israel. They can be considered, according to Sumpter, "a minority within a minority within a minority".[43] The State of Israel has almost nine million residents of which twenty percent is Arab. Around 10 percent of them are Christian which constitutes around 160,00 individuals. The majority of them reside in the north of Israel. Due to economic, political and religious pressures, Arab Christians in the Holy Land have emigrated to the West by the masses since the beginning of the twentieth century. Subsequently, more than 250,000 of them – including those of evangelical faith – live in the diaspora.[44] Although the number of Arab Christians in Israel and the Middle East is decreasing rapidly, there is still a Christian presence in the country and region where the gospel was first preached.[45]

2.3   Muslim-Background Believers

With the exodus of Arab Christians from the Middle East, there is a surprising countermovement emerging from among Arab Muslims in the region and beyond. For the first time in history, they are coming to faith in large numbers and, according to a recent survey, there might be as many as half a million Arab Muslims around the world who have decided to become Jesus followers.[46] These numbers seem to be confirmed by a recent study of Garrison in which he claims that between two to seven million Muslims have been baptised worldwide since the beginning of the twenty-first century.[47] Although these reports have to be received with a certain level of caution, there seems to be a remarkable growth of Jesus followers in the House of Islam'. Throughout Church history – from Francis of Assisi in Egypt in the thirteenth century to Protestant mission workers in the Levant in the nineteenth century – there has never been such a widespread movement of Muslims coming to faith in Christ as witnessed today –

---

[43]   Ajaj, Miller, and Sumpter, 38.

[44]   Bailey and Bailey, *Who Are the Christians in the Middle East?*, 156.

[45]   According to Garrison, "more than five percent of the population in the Middle East are Christian". This is a significant decline from the twenty percent mentioned before by the turn of the nineteenth century. David Garrison, *A Wind in the House of Islam: How God Is Drawing Muslims around the World to Faith in Jesus Christ* (Monument, CO: WIGTake Resources, 2014), 208.

[46]   These figures from Miller are derived from his personal contact with Patrick Johnstone who is "one of the world's foremost experts on mission and Christian demographics". Miller, *Living among the Breakage*, 83–85.

[47]   Garrison, *A Wind in the House of Islam*, 5.

according to Garrison.[48] As Arab Christianity in the Middle East is threatened by extinction, a new community of evangelical faith is emerging in the region.

In Israel and the West Bank there have also been reports of Muslims coming to faith. According to a recent study by Miller, there are around 500 Muslim-background believers in the Holy Land.[49] Although the number is small, he argues that "it has grown substantially in the last two decades".[50] Some of these Jesus followers find their way to Evangelical churches or Messianic congregations, but a large number remains unaffiliated. To some extent, this is related to the cold welcome they receive from the local churches. In the West Bank, clergy will not baptise believers with a Muslim background because of the political and societal pressures they face. In Jerusalem this does not seem to be an issue as Israeli citizens have the right to change their religion under the law of the State. However, priests from traditional churches warn these Jesus followers that they will encounter persecution from their friends and family members if they go public with their newly-found faith. Miller suggests that Muslim-background believers should be received with open arms by Evangelical churches even though sensitivity is required for their safety and practical needs. In the end, they might turn out to be a lifeline for the Church in the Middle East.

This chapter has provided a historical overview of the birth and growth of three communities of evangelical faith in the Holy Land. This raises the question: what do they have in common to justify a comparative study?

---

48 Garrison, 6–15.

49 This number is disputed by one of the interviewees (MBB2), he claims that there are only fifty in the Holy Land. From his own research, the author of this thesis reckons that the number of Miller is not too far off. Duane Alexander Miller, 'Christians from a Muslim Background in the Middle East', in *Routledge Handbook of Minorities in the Middle East*, ed. Paul S. Rowe, Routledge Handbooks (London ; New York, NY: Routledge/Taylor & Francis Group, 2019), 133.

50 Ajaj, Miller, and Sumpter, *Arab Evangelicals in Israel*, 92–99.

3: Points of Commonality

From the historical overview of the three targets groups, it could be argued that there is some level of commonality between these communities of evangelical faith. This chapter seeks to address the question regarding what exactly they have in common and how this justifies a comparative study.[51]

3.1 Country of Residency

Members of the target groups share, first and foremost, residence of the same country – namely the State of Israel. Therefore, they have lived through similar societal changes and political upheavals in recent decades. Although the effect of these events on their personal lives might be different – which could have an influence on the way they interpret them – they share common experiences as members of Israeli society. An illustration of this phenomenon can be found in "The Land Cries Out" by Salim Munayer and Lisa Loden.[52] A wide-range of theologians from the Holy Land share their views in this book on the 'promise of the land'. However, for most of them it is not merely a theological question but also an issue that is deeply personal. Some of them moved to the 'land of their fathers' while others were forcefully removed from the 'land of their ancestors'. Subsequently, they might view the creation of the State of Israel very differently, but – at the same time – they are formed and shaped by the same events as residences of the Holy Land. This is true – to a greater or lesser extent – for all members of the target groups on a wide range of political matters and societal issues.

3.2 Language, Culture and Worldview

A point of commonality that could be easily neglected is that those belonging to these target groups share more than one common language. Even though Hebrew is the main language in Messianic congregations and

---

[51] It should be noted that there are, of course, also differences between these three target groups. However, it is beyond the scope of this thesis to discuss each one of them. Therefore, they will be only be addressed if they are related to the central research question and sub-questions.

[52] Salim Munayer and Lisa Loden, *The Land Cries out: Theology of the Land in the Israeli-Palestinian Context* (Eugene, Or.: Cascade Books, 2012).

Arabic in the Arab Evangelical churches, quite a number of their members are able to communicate in both languages.[53] In addition, English is widely spoken among believers of evangelical faith in the Holy Land because of their close relationship with believers from abroad. This became evident, for example, in the research conducted by Dunning among Muslim-background believers in the West-Bank. He was surprised to find out that many of them answered the questions in either Hebrew or English and, at times, even preferred to use these languages as a sign of courtesy towards him.[54] Besides the fact that most members of the target groups are bilingual or trilingual, they are also used to finding a common language when they meet at prayer meetings and conferences. Generally speaking, this is either English or Hebrew.[55] Furthermore, as pointed out before, a number of theological issues are discussed in books in which English is used as a common language. In this way, the voices of believers from the Holy Land are heard by evangelicals around the world. In addition, the theological matters discussed can be included in the academic discourse. In conclusion, common languages – most notably; Hebrew, Arabic and English – provide a means for members of the target groups to communicate with one another in a language that is close to their heart.

Two out of the three languages that believers of evangelical faith in Israel have in common are considered Semitic. This is more significant than one might realise initially because a large number of words are 'borrowed' from either languages. For this reason, there is a sense of belonging between these Semitic languages. This might serve as an illustration of a wider phenomenon observable in Israeli society which is sometimes sidelined in academic research on these target groups. Due to their ethnic, cultural and historical background, they have more in common than is often recognised. Shared values – such as, the importance of the 'collective' over the 'individual' – are clearly observable among all members of the three targets groups. Furthermore, at a deeper level, their worldviews are also

---

[53] According to the survey conducted by Soref, ninety-two percent of the messianic congregations consider Hebrew their main language in their services. Similarly, Ajaj and Sumpter indicate that Arabic is the main language of internal communication in the CICE. Soref, 'The Messianic Jewish Movement in Modern Israel', 143.; Ajaj, Miller, and Sumpter, Arab Evangelicals in Israel, 37.

[54] Dunning was not able to converse in Arabic and, therefore, the interviews were conducted in either Hebrew or English in order to benefit from not having to rely on a translator. Dunning, 'Palestinian Muslims Converting to Christianity: Effective Evangelistic Methods in the West Bank.', 158.

[55] It should be noted, that translation into various languages is commonly provided at these occasions.

similar with regards to topics like 'shame and honour'.[56] Although much more could be said about what they have in common in the area of language, culture and worldviews – similar to those who reside in the Holy Land but do not belong to the target groups – the following section will now focus on the faith they share as Jesus followers.

3.3   The Protestant Mission

The revival movements that swept through Britain and North America during the eighteenth and nineteenth century, has had a profound effect on believers in the Holy Land. Due to these awakenings, as pointed out before, societies were formed "specifically devoted to foreign mission".[57] Mission workers were also commissioned to the Holy Land to share the gospel with Jews and Muslims. Due to the limited success among these two groups, they also started to reach out to members of the Orthodox and Catholic churches.[58] From this moment onwards, Protestant mission workers have played a major role in the development of communities of evangelical faith in the Holy Land. This is most noticeable in the church denominations present in the Arab Evangelical community, such as Baptist and Assemblies of God churches.[59] The same can be observed among the Messianic movement in Israel although it is not as prominent or public. In addition, many pastors have received their training through evangelical seminaries in Europe and North America. As expected, this has had a major effect on theology-making in the Holy Land. Lastly, there is still a significant number of congregations that receive funding – although less than before – by individuals and organisations from abroad.[60] For all these reasons, Protestant mission has played a major role in the birth and growth of these communities of evangelical faith in Israel and, therefore, can be considered a third point of commonality among the target groups.

---

[56]   Dunning, 'Palestinian Muslims Converting to Christianity: Effective Evangelistic Methods in the West Bank.', 43–46.

[57]   Bosch, *Transforming Mission*, 281.

[58]   As pointed out before, Israeli Jews eventually became interested in the gospel during the second half of the twentieth century and – more recently – Muslims in the Holy Land have come to faith in Jesus as well. Since the turn of the millennium, one could argue that there are three indigenous communities of evangelical faith present in the State of Israel.

[59]   Ajaj, Miller, and Sumpter, *Arab Evangelicals in Israel*, 35.

[60]   Soref, 'The Messianic Jewish Movement in Modern Israel', 143.

3.4   Religious Minority Group

Although the number of believers of evangelical faith in the Holy Land has grown in recent decades – most notably among MJs and MBBs – they are still considered a minority group within Israeli society. Consequently, members of these target groups experience similar struggles and challenges in their daily lives – this is the fourth point of commonality. Arab Evangelicals, for example, face pressure from the Jewish government as well as the Muslim community.[61] In addition, they are ill-treated by members of the traditional churches because of their evangelical faith. In a similar way, Messianic Jews face hostility from Orthodox Jews and – although less than before – Israeli society due to their faith in Jesus the Messiah.[62] Therefore, those belonging to these two target groups go through similar experiences – according to Kjaer-Hansen – because "the collective sense of any minority is to feel pushed out and marginalized in relation to the larger context in which they live and function. Believers in Jesus, whatever their identification, also feel this marginalization."[63] From this perspective, Muslim-background believers are in an even more challenging position because they are often isolated from their community of birth as well as traditional and evangelical churches. Miller calls them, therefore, "marginal believers".[64] Although the experiences of Messianic Jews, Arab Evangelicals and Muslim-background believers are different in terms of intensity they are all exposed to "resentment, fear, suspicion, bitterness, and a downward spiral of indignity" as members of a minority group.[65]

3.5   Believers of Evangelical Faith

The fifth point of commonality among members of the target groups is that they are considered believers of evangelical faith by outsiders. Although there are a number of arguments to identify them as such – as already discussed in §1.5 – it should be noted that the label 'evangelical' is

---

[61]   Ajaj, Miller, and Sumpter, *Arab Evangelicals in Israel*, 87–88.
[62]   More than forty percent of Jesus-believing Jews has experienced some form of persecution, according to a recent survey, because of their connection to the Messianic movement. At the same time, they also expressed in the questionnaire that their presence in Israeli society is more tolerated than ever before. Soref, 'The Messianic Jewish Movement in Modern Israel', 146, 149.
[63]   Kjaer-Hansen, *Jewish Identity and Faith in Jesus*, 109.
[64]   Ajaj, Miller, and Sumpter, *Arab Evangelicals in Israel*, 92.
[65]   Kjaer-Hansen, *Jewish Identity and Faith in Jesus*, 108.

not widely accepted by Messianic Jews and Muslim-background believers and can even be considered problematic for a number of reasons.

For Jesus-believing Jews this label is often offensive, because it connects them directly to Christianity. As "terminology has considerable theological significance", they prefer to identify themselves by their ethnicity and their faith in the Messiah rather than being associated with the "legacy of Christian anti-Semitism and anti-Judaism" – according to Harvey.[66] The extent to which they are part of Judaism is widely-debated, although there seems to be some consensus that the term 'Messianic Judaism' refers to the collective body of Jesus-believing Jews within the people of Israel.[67] Interestingly, a recent survey showed that Messianic Jews "identify significantly with both the Jewish world, and only slightly less with the evangelical world, simultaneously."[68] Regardless of these sensitivities, Messianic Jews are often called 'evangelicals' or 'evangelical Protestants' by those outside of the community – for example by Bailey and Bailey – but this will not be the case in this thesis.[69]

For Muslim-background believers in the Middle East, the label 'evangelical' – and more generally 'Christian' – is not easily adopted because of the "welcome" they have received by church members. According to Kraft, they often feel that the members do not trust them and, as a result, eventually leave these churches.[70] This is a cause for great disappointment, because they have often paid a high price for leaving the 'Muslim umma' – which refers to "the unity of the community of Islam" – and are looking for a 'Christian umma'.[71] Although there is no data available to confirm if this is also the case for Muslim-background believers in the Holy Land, it is not unreasonable to assume that this might also be their experience. It is for this reason that they will not be called 'evangelical' or 'Christian' by the author of this thesis.

For Arab Evangelicals – as the name already suggests – the term 'evangelical' is less problematic. Arguably, it is even an identity marker to set them apart from nominal Christians – i.e. non-evangelical members of the traditional churches. However, they also experience tension between their community of birth and their community of evangelical faith. According

---

[66] Richard Harvey, *Mapping Messianic Jewish Theology: A Constructive Approach*, Studies in Messianic Jewish Theology (Milton Keynes, U.K: Paternoster, 2009), 9.

[67] Harvey, 11.

[68] Soref, 'The Messianic Jewish Movement in Modern Israel', 145.

[69] Bailey and Bailey, *Who Are the Christians in the Middle East?*, 53, 152.

[70] Kathryn Ann Kraft, *Searching for Heaven in the Real World: A Sociological Discussion of Conversion in the Arab World.* (Cork: Words By Design, 2013), 56–58.

[71] Kraft, 47.

to Miller, Arab Evangelicals "can be subjected to verbal attacks from the traditional churches, who often associate them with Zionists" and – at the same time – they feel forgotten by the evangelical family around the world because they often relate more readily to Messianic Jews in Israel.[72] Arab Evangelicals find themselves, therefore, in the middle of two communities who do not fully embrace them. As such, the word 'evangelical' refers no longer to the original meaning in Arabic – i.e. 'gospel' – but has become a divisive term.

It is perhaps surprising how similar these experiences are among members of the three target groups. Due to their newly-found faith they are, to some extent, disconnected from their communities of birth and, at the same time, do not feel fully part of the global evangelical community. Naturally, one might assume that these communities could replace one another but this does not seem to be the case among members of all the three target groups. This is another experience they have in common.

Based on these observations, the question could be asked whether members of the target groups can truly be called 'evangelical', especially as the majority of them do not want to be identified as such.[73] Without going into detail about the sociological issue of self-identification – this topic will be addressed later in chapter 4 – there is one essential element to the evangelical faith which is commonly experienced by Messianic Jews, Arab Evangelicals and Muslim-background believers, namely the life-changing encounter with the person of Jesus. This "change of hearts and lives", as Bosch calls it, was the main driving force behind the Protestant mission and became a prominent feature of evangelical faith.[74] According to Cumming, evangelicals are not primarily concerned if people call themselves Christian but "whether one has life-transformation relationship with Jesus Christ."[75] Similarly, Stern points out that the contemporary understanding of conversion refers to 'changing religious community', but from a biblical point of view means "coming to genuine faith in *Yeshua* the Messiah".[76] Therefore, it could be argued that it is not relevant whether members of the target groups identify themselves as 'evangelical' and/or members of their religion of birth, but – based on their 'change of hearts and lives' and

---

[72]   Ajaj, Miller, and Sumpter, *Arab Evangelicals in Israel*, 97.
[73]   For reasons mentioned above, the author of this thesis has decided to use this label only for Arab Evangelicals.
[74]   Bosch, *Transforming Mission*, 288.
[75]   Harley Talman and John Travis, eds., *Understanding Insider Movements: Disciples of Jesus within Diverse Religious Communities* (Pasadena, CA: William Carey Library, 2015), 28.
[76]   Stern, *Messianic Jewish Manifesto*, 80.

'coming to faith in Jesus' – they can be considered 'believers of evangelical faith'.[77] This is the fifth point of commonality among Messianic Jews, Arab Evangelicals and Muslims-background believers in Israel.

3.6   Missiological Interest

The points of commonality among believers of evangelical faith in the Holy Land, mentioned above, have not remained unnoticed by local theologians as well as missiologists in the West. Due to their interest in seeing the Kingdom of God advance in Israel and the Middle East, some have compared the experiences of members of these target groups in order to gain new insights on evangelism, discipleship and church planting. This missiological interest is the sixth and final commonality that believers of evangelical faith in Israel share as members of these target groups.

In recent decades, the main topic of interest has been around 'contextualisation'. In brief, there are a number of key points that need to be mentioned with regard to this highly debated issue within the field of missiology. First, Kraft and subsequently, Cole and Travis argue that Messianic Judaism can serve as a model for 'Messianic Muslims' to combine their newly-found faith with redeemable elements of Islam.[78] In these studies, the comparison is often made with the first disciples of Jesus who followed him within the context of Second Temple Judaism.[79] Joshua Massey goes even further by arguing that mission workers that serve in Islamic countries should keep the Law – in accordance with the interpretation given by Jesus and the first apostles – in order to reach devout Muslims effectively.[80] From a slightly different perspective, Van de Poll presents the holiday

---

[77]   During the interviews, interestingly, members of the target groups often called themselves and the members of the other target groups 'believers'.

[78]   Mark Durie, 'Messianic Judaism and Deliverance', in *Muslim Conversions to Christ: A Critique of Insider Movements in Islamic Contexts*, ed. Ayman S. Ibrahim and Ant B. Greenham (New York: Peter Lang, 2018), 265–67.

[79]   The following four essays discus this issue in length and are either in favour or opposition of this proposition: Richard Jameson and Nick Scalevich, 'First-Century Jews and Twentieth-Century Muslims', *International Journal of Frontier Missiology* 17, no. 1 (2000): 33–39.; Talman and Travis, *Understanding Insider Movements*, 249 –261.; Durie, 'Messianic Judaism and Deliverance', 267–68.; Talman and Travis, *Understanding Insider Movements*, 497–99.

[80]   Joshua Massey, 'Part I – Living like Jesus, a Torah-Observant Jew: Delighting in God's Law for Incarnational Witness to Muslims', *International Journal of Frontier Missiology* 21, no. 1 (2004): 13–22.; Joshua Massey, 'Part II – Living like Jesus, a Torah-Observant Jew: Delighting in God's Law for Incarnational Witness to Muslims', *International Journal of Frontier Missiology* 21, no. 2 (2004): 55–71.

practice of Messianic Jews as an example of 'inculturation' – C4 within
Travis' model of contextualisation – and suggests that further research
needs to be done if this form of indigenous worship can also be used for
evangelism among Muslims.[81] Although others – most notably, Mark Durie
– are not convinced that Messianic Judaism can serve as model for contextualisation among Muslim-background believers, the topic has drawn
much missiological interest.[82]

To a lesser extent, the topic of conversion has been researched among
the three monotheistic religions. Lewis Rambo provides, for example, an
overview of the conversion processes and experiences in Judaism, Christianity and Islam.[83] However, there is – as of present – no comparative study
available which focusses specifically on the three target groups.[84] Notably,
the same is true for the topic of identity formation.[85] As stated before, this
thesis will be a first attempt to compare the personal and collective experiences of Messianic Jews, Arab Evangelicals and Muslim-background believers – with regards to their identity formation – by bringing together
research and field studies conducted on the members of these target
groups.[86]

In this chapter, it has been contended that Messianic Jews, Arab Evangelicals and Muslim-background Believers in Israel have much in common
due to their country of residence, language, culture and worldview. In

---

[81]   Van de Poll, *Sacred Times for Chosen People*, 320, 359.
[82]   Largely based on Telchin's observations, Durie concludes that a strong emphasis
       on Rabbinic Judaism has proven to be an ineffective tool for reaching Jews with
       the gospel. Durie, 'Messianic Judaism and Deliverance', 267–70.
[83]   Lewis R. Rambo, ed., *The Oxford Handbook of Religious Conversion* (Oxford ; New York:
       Oxford University Press, 2014), 578–686.
[84]   Greenham seems to be the only one who has suggested that the conversion expe-
       riences of Palestinian converts should be compared with converted Jews in Israel.
       Greenham, 'Muslim Conversions to Christ: An Investigation of Palestinian Con-
       verts Living in the Holy Land', 235.
[85]   To the author's knowledge, there is only one study that has compared the identity
       formation of Jews, Muslims and Christians. However, the focus of Reedijk's disser-
       tation is on the experiences of those who participate in interreligious dialogue –
       also called 'boundary-dwellers' – rather than Jesus followers from these back-
       grounds. W Reedijk, 'Roots and Routes: Identity Construction and the Jewish-
       Christian-Muslim Dialogue' (Amsterdam, Vrije Universiteit Amsterdam, 2010).
[86]   Only after the completion of this thesis, the author became aware of a book writ-
       ten by Loden and Munayer in which they discuss the identity formation of Messi-
       anic Jews and Palestinian Christians in relation to reconciliation. Although their
       findings could not be discussed anymore in this thesis, they should be included in
       further research on this topic. Salim Munayer and Lisa Loden, *Through My Enemy's
       Eyes: Envisioning Reconciliation in Israel-Palestine*, 2014.

addition, it has been argued that they share parts of the same history and encounter similar issues in their daily lives as the 'spiritual fruit' of the Protestant mission in the Holy Land. Therefore, members of the target groups have enough in common to justify a comparative study between these communities of evangelical faith.

4: Identity Formation

Even though the identity formation of members of the target groups has not been compared in academic studies, the topic itself has been extensively researched among Messianic Jews, Arab Evangelicals and Muslim-background believers separately. In this chapter, an overview will be provided of the main findings of academic research and field studies conducted in recent years.[87]

4.1 Messianic Jews

According to Richard Harvey "more than twenty significant studies of Messianic Judaism have appeared since the 1970s" from scholars in the field of anthropology, social psychology and historical theology.[88] The topic of identity formation is frequently addressed in their research but, more often than not, related to Jesus-believing Jews in North America. Nevertheless, some of the findings are relevant to the central research question of this thesis and, therefore, a brief summary of the main points will be presented.

4.1.1 Boundary Crossing and Boundary Marking

The most well-known study is, arguably, Feher's research into the construction of boundaries within Messianic Judaism. From an anthropological point of view, she suggests that Jesus-believing Jews are trying to find 'a third way' because they are, first of all, constantly crossing the well-established borders between Judaism and Christianity and, secondly, marking new boundaries between Messianic Judaism and these two religions.[89] Although her findings cannot be generalised, as pointed out by Van de Poll, they provide an interesting insight into how Messianic Jews are trying to negotiate their dual-belonging to the Church and the people of Israel.[90]

---

87 The order of presentation will be from *general* to *specific, past* to *present, global* to *local*.

88 Harvey, *Mapping Messianic Jewish Theology*, 14.

89 Shoshanah Feher, *Passing over Easter: Constructing the Boundaries of Messianic Judaism* (Walnut Creek, CA: AltaMira Press, 1998), 75–95.

90 According to Van de Poll, the findings of his own research demonstrate that Messianic Jews are not trying to find a 'third way' but observe the Jewish holidays in order to be part of and make the gospel accessible to their kinsman. In view of

Stern describes this tension as follows: "I have two hats, I am part of two communities at odds with each other."[91] As demonstrated by Harvey, the formation of a "hybridised but independent religious identity, building a tradition that is both Jewish and Christian" has been researched by a number of scholars – he discusses the findings of Senay, Harris-Shapiro, Berger and Cohen – although their studies seem to be less influential in the academic debate than the research of Feher.[92]

Most of these scholars start and, ultimately, return to the question of "what does it mean to be Jewish?" Within Judaism, there is no consensus as to who is a Jew but it is generally accepted that those who believe in Jesus are no longer considered Jews.[93] This view however is challenged by Messianic Jews. Stern argues, for example, that Jesus-believing Jews are 100% Jewish and 100% Messianic.[94] From a theological point of view, he notes that the first believers remained ethnic Jews when they became Jesus followers and, hence, there is no requirement for Jews today to become 'gentile Christians' if they accept Jesus as their Messiah. However, there remains an underlying question around the extent to which the term 'Jewishness' refers to faith, culture and/or nation. These used to be the three core elements of Judaism, according to Warshawsky, but "Jewish people today are much freer than ever to shift, choose and interpret the components of their Jewish identity" because of "the ideological movement and freedoms introduced by the Enlightenment."[95] Hence, Messianic Jews are part of this quest to define 'Jewishness'. In his research, Van de Poll claims that Jesus-believing Jews identify themselves – first and foremost – ethnically and culturally as Jews rather than identifying themselves religiously.[96] In doing so, they challenge the common notion that Rabbinic Judaism is the norm for 'Jewishness' and, simultaneously, they refuse to

---

this, the holiday practice of Jesus-believing Jews serves as an identity and cultural affinity marker – rather than a boundary marker – to the Jewish community. At the same, he recognises that the Christological interpretation of the biblical feasts does create borders between them and adherents of Rabbinic Judaism in the same way that the observance of the biblical holidays forms a boundary between them and Evangelicals. Van de Poll, *Sacred Times for Chosen People*, 270, 338–54.

91 Stern, *Messianic Jewish Manifesto*, 26.
92 Harvey, *Mapping Messianic Jewish Theology*, 19.
93 Keri Zelson Warshawsky, 'Returning To Their Own Borders; A Social Anthropological Study of Contemporary Messianic Jewish Identity in Israel' (Jerusalem, The Hebrew University, 2008), 1.
94 Stern, *Messianic Jewish Manifesto*, 24.
95 Warshawsky, 'Returning To Their Own Borders; A Social Anthropological Study of Contemporary Messianic Jewish Identity in Israel', 38.
96 Van de Poll, *Sacred Times for Chosen People*, 112.

accept that their faith in Jesus is a boundary marker between them and their fellow Jews.[97]

The studies discussed so far are predominately concerned with boundary crossing and boundary marking of Messianic Jews throughout the world. However, these issues are – to some extent – removed from the everyday experiences of Jesus-believing Jews in Israel. In the second part of this overview on the identity formation of Messianic Jews, recent surveys and field studies among members of the target group will be presented and discussed.

4.1.2 Surveys from 1999 and 2017

Twenty years ago, Kjær-Hansen conducted with Bodil Skjøtt a survey – the first of its kind – among congregational leaders in Israel. Although their research was mainly focussed on generating data about Messianic congregations, they observed that there was a noticeable increase of Jewish expression and identity among the members.[98] However, they did not detect any changes in their theology or a growing affiliation to synagogues. Even though the survey of Kjaer-Hansen and Skjøtt provides a meaningful insight into the characteristics of the Messianic movement in Israel, Warshawsky makes an important point by drawing attention to the fact that the results of the survey do not reflect "the everyday life, opinions, decisions and identity struggles of the individual Messianic Jew in context."[99]

Possibly with this point of criticism in mind, Soref conducted a similar survey in 2017.[100] Close to three hundred participants, both leaders and members of Messianic congregations, filled out a questionnaire in either Hebrew, English or Russian. The data generated from this research project is rich and diverse in content.

With regards to identity formation, the researchers note that "while the Messianic Jewish identity in Israel is likely to continue to evolve in the coming decades, a level of stability in terms of presence in society seems to have been achieved."[101] This observation suggests that the position of Jesus-believing Jews as members of Israeli society has significantly

---

[97]   Van de Poll, 343.
[98]   Kai Kjaer-Hansen and Bodil F. Skjøtt, *Facts & Myths about Messianic Congregations in Israel*, Miskan 30–31 (Jerusalem: United Christian Council in Israel, 1999), 28–29.
[99]   Warshawsky, 'Returning To Their Own Borders; A Social Anthropological Study of Contemporary Messianic Jewish Identity in Israel', 3.
[100] Soref, 'The Messianic Jewish Movement in Modern Israel', 141–50.
[101] Soref, 149.

improved in recent decades. However, the researchers point out as well that Messianic Jews still face various forms of rejection and persecution because of their faith in Jesus. This is a real challenge for them as they identify – ideologically, religiously and practically – with the people of Israel and are, at the same time, rejected by this community.[102] This could be the reason, as aforementioned in §3.5, why the majority of Jesus-believing Jews in Israel identify themselves with the Jewish community as well as the Evangelical world.[103]

Lastly, the survey shows that the majority of Messianic Jews in Israel only observe biblical holidays and do not add much value to religious symbols – i.e. the menorah or Torah scrolls – in their congregations.[104] This might be an indication that they largely prefer to stay away from Rabbinic Judaism in their practice and expression of faith in Jesus. Nevertheless, the majority of participants view their congregation as Israeli both in character and culture. This seems to confirm the notion that Messianic Jews view their 'Jewishness' – first and foremost – ethnically and culturally rather than religiously as argued by Van de Poll (§4.1.1).

4.1.3 Identity-as-Travel

Thus far, only one field study has been conducted on the issue of identity formation among Jesus-believing Jews in Israel.[105] Based on sixty semi-structured interviews with Israeli Messianic Jews, Warshawsky provides a thorough and in-depth overview of some of the main challenges they

---

[102] Soref, 145.

[103] Unfortunately, there is no data provided on how many participants are considered Jewish according to the criteria of the State of Israel – i.e. through the bloodline of the mother or conversion to Orthodox Judaism. From a personal conversation with one of the assistant researchers (Karen Silver) the author found out that a large number of participants had either a Jewish father or mother.

[104] Although the survey did not ask about their views on the Christian holidays and symbols, it is well-documented that Messianic Jews usually refrain from these expressions of evangelical faith. Soref, 'The Messianic Jewish Movement in Modern Israel', 143–45.

[105] More recently, a second field study was published by a postgraduate student from the University of Oslo. Although the findings are interesting, they cannot be considered representative for the community of Messianic Jews in Israel due to the limited number of interviews conducted. Christine Eidsheim, 'Negotiating a Messianic Identity: A Study on the Formation of Messianic Identity through Space, Art, and Language in Modern Israel [Unpublished Thesis]' (Oslo, University of Oslo, 2019).

encounter in their daily lives.[106] She is very critical of the studies mentioned above, because she finds them narrow in scope, based on little evidence, driven by a 'hidden agenda' and removed from every day practice.[107] Therefore, the aim of her research is to let Israeli Messianic Jews "speak for themselves as much as possible, and to remain true to the intent, content and context of their message."[108]

From a social anthropological perspective, Warshawsky points out that identity should not be perceived as *static* but *fluid* and, as such, it is more about *becoming* than *being*.[109] This seems to be confirmed by her research, as the majority of interviewees "narrate their faith journeys as a process of returning home to Zion – a composite unity of God, the land and the Jewish birthright."[110] In this endeavour, they construct their 'identity-as-travel' through *routes*, *roots* and *borders*.[111]

The first identity paradigm – i.e. routes – refers to their experience of returning to the God of Israel by coming to faith in Messiah Jesus. Interestingly, there seems to be a tension between the *narrated* "spiral construct of the Messianic faith journey" and the *experienced* "hegemonic linear interpretation of 'conversion'."[112] In other words, Jesus-believing Jews *say* that they have been through a 'renewal' as Jews but they *encounter* 'newness' as Messianic Jews.[113] For this reason, they follow the Christian and Jewish paradigm of 'coming to faith' – i.e. 'newness' – rather than through their suggested paradigm of 'returning to Zion' – i.e. 'renewal'. According to Warshawsky, this is an indication that Israeli Messianic Jews view their 'Jewishness' ultimately as their national rather than their religious identity.

The second identity paradigm – i.e. roots – is related to the longing of Messianic Jews to express their faith independently and indigenously despite the "ongoing influences of secular Israeli culture, orthodox Judaism,

---

[106] Warshawsky, 'Returning To Their Own Borders; A Social Anthropological Study of Contemporary Messianic Jewish Identity in Israel'.

[107] Warshawsky, 2–5.

[108] Warshawsky, 10.

[109] Warshawsky, 12–14.

[110] Warshawsky, 58.

[111] Warshawsky, 59.

[112] Warshawsky, 201.

[113] According to Lewis R. Rambo, it is common for converts to reinterpret their past experiences based on the terminology they learn in their new religious community. As such, they tend to reconstruct their biography in order to be able to share a testimony that is acceptable by the other converts. This might be an explanation why Warshawsky detected a difference between the *experienced* and *narrated* process of conversion. Rambo, *Understanding Religious Conversion*, 118–21, 137–41.

the Protestant mission, Christian Zionism and western consumer colonial-
ism."[114] Some examples have already been provided in the previous chapter, such as; the influence of Evangelicalism on the Messianic movement
in Israel. This issue is also noticeable, for example, with the Law of Return
– the right of any Jew to move back to the land of their fathers – in the
State of Israel. According to a strict interpretation of the *halakhah* – i.e.
Jewish Law – Jesus-believing Jews are no longer considered Jews because
they have converted to Christianity and, for this reason, they have lost
their right to immigrate to Israel.[115] Although more secular voices within
Israeli society argue that 'Jewishness' should not be defined by religion but
rather by ethnicity, this remains an unresolved matter. This issue is a
prime example of the numerous challenges encountered by Jesus-believing Jews in returning to the roots of their faith, both geographically and
spiritually.

The third identity paradigm – i.e. borders – refers to the struggle of
Messianic Jews to define and mark their own territory as a unique movement of Jesus-followers throughout history to the present day. In doing so,
they have to continue drawing boundaries and operate autonomously
within the Jewish world and the Evangelical community.[116] According to
Warshawky, this is because "a battle rages over the legitimacy and expression of the Israeli Messianic Jewish faith community", however she also
notes that "one of the strengths of the emergent Israeli Messianic Jewish
modality is its maintenance of the dynamic tension between total segrega-
tion from and complete assimilation into the larger Jewish and "Messianic" communities."[117] The challenge of boundary crossing and boundary
marking, as mentioned in §4.1.1, is also present among Jesus-believing
Jews in Israel and, as such, the field study of Warshawsky seems to confirm
the earlier findings of Feher.

4.2   Arab Evangelicals

The number of field studies on the identity formation of Arab Evangelicals
in Israel is limited, but more data is available on Palestinian Christians in

---

[114]   Warshawsky, 'Returning To Their Own Borders; A Social Anthropological Study of
        Contemporary Messianic Jewish Identity in Israel', 202.
[115]   According to Jewish Law, those who have a Jewish mother or converted to Judaism
        are considered Jews. This definition has been adopted by the State of Israel. Kjaer-
        Hansen, *Jewish Identity and Faith in Jesus*, 79–86.
[116]   Warshawsky, 'Returning To Their Own Borders; A Social Anthropological Study of
        Contemporary Messianic Jewish Identity in Israel', 202–3.
[117]   Warshawsky, 220.

the Holy Land with regards to their ethnic and social identity as a religious minority group.

4.2.1 Historical Changes in the Arab Christian Identity

With the turn of the twentieth century, Muslims and Christians started to identify themselves mainly by their shared ethnicity and nationality as Arabs. Religious beliefs and affiliation were reduced to private matters, but their 'Arabness' was considered a unifying factor for their people group. Interestingly, Christians were the forerunners of this social change in the Middle East. They believed that it might open the door for them to become "equal participants within the broader community".[118] However, Arab Christians could not have foreseen the socio-religious changes that would occur in the Holy Land, namely the Judaisation of Israeli society and the Islamisation of Palestinian society.[119]

From his literature review and field study, Sumpter provides a number of useful illustrations to demonstrate the particularly difficult position of Arab Christians in Israeli society.[120] As a minority group, they do not share the same history as the Jewish people and, therefore, they cannot relate to – for example – the national anthem of the State Israel which recalls the yearning for Zion by those living in exile. Other illustrations are provided by Sumpter in which the same issues emerge, such as: enlisting in the IDF, participating in Israeli elections, and celebrating national holidays. Similar problems – which are directly related to their status as a minority group – also emerge in Arab Israeli society, especially with regards to the cities and towns that were once considered Christian. Not long ago, Sumpter recalls, Muslims built a mosque in front of the Catholic basilica, posted hateful messages towards non-believers on billboards and attacked Christians both verbally and physically in Nazareth, the hometown of Jesus. Although Arab Christians have always been a minority group in the Holy land, the pressure they face has significantly increased in recent decades – according to Sumpter. Consequently, many of them have emigrated to countries

---

[118] Ajaj, Miller, and Sumpter, *Arab Evangelicals in Israel*, 8.

[119] Although Calder provides limited evidence for this claim, he argues that the Israeli government actively denies the 'Arabness' of Christians by some of their state policies and that Palestinian politicians do not prevent the changing societal and religious norms with regards to the observance of Islamic festivals and conservative dress code. Mark Daniel Calder, 'Palestinian Christians – Situating Selves in a Dislocated Present', in *Routledge Handbook of Minorities in the Middle East*, ed. Paul S. Rowe, Routledge Handbooks (London ; New York, NY: Routledge, 2019), 106–7.

[120] Ajaj, Miller, and Sumpter, *Arab Evangelicals in Israel*, 10–34.

in the West where "Arabs are not stuck in an ethnic or religious box which is then negatively evaluated" by their fellow citizens.[121] Psychological reasons play, possibly even more than economic reasons, a major role in the exodus of Arab Christians from the Holy Land.[122]

In sum, Sumpter's literature review and fieldwork contend that Arab Christians feel increasingly threatened as a minority group within Israeli and Palestinian society and, as a result, there is "a growing trend of Christians realigning themselves with the religious rather than national communities."[123] Based on these observations, Sumpter concludes that the main identity of Arab Christians in the Holy Land has moved from *Arab* to *Christian* in the twentieth century. Based on this observation, it might be considered more appropriate to call them 'Christian Arabs'.

4.2.2 Integration of Palestinian Arab Christian Adolescents in Israel

The primary aim of Salim Munayer's field study among Palestinian adolescents in Israel is to unravel the complexity of the Arab Christian identity.[124] From the perspective of social and developmental psychology, he conducted a quantitative research project in the Holy Land back in 1999. From his findings, he concludes that the participants viewed their social ethnic identity as *distinct* and *positive*.[125] Although they experience pressure from both Jews and Muslims to assimilate into their societies, they prefer to only integrate and – simultaneously – remain separated. Interestingly, they placed *integration* before *separation* with regards to Jewish society but gave the reverse order concerning Muslim society. This might be, according to Munayer, due to their longing for Westernisation – in which the State of Israel serves as a 'means to an end' – and their negative experiences as

---

[121] Ajaj, Miller, and Sumpter, 23.
[122] Another phenomenon that has recently been witnessed in the Holy Land is that Christians no longer identify themselves as Arabs, but as Arabic-speakers from another ethnic background – such as, Aramaic or Maronite. In this way, they feel that they can integrate more fully in Israeli society and, subsequently, feel less pressure to move abroad. Ajaj, Miller, and Sumpter, 31.
[123] Interestingly, Arab Christians in Israel seem to be more confident that they can receive equal status as citizens in a Jewish State than in a Islamic society. Ajaj, Miller, and Sumpter, 33.
[124] Salim Munayer, 'The Ethnic Identity of Palestinian Arab Christian Adolescents in Israel' (Oxford, Oxford Centre for Mission Studies, 2000).
[125] Munayer, 110–21.

second class citizens under Islamic rule over the last thirteen centuries.[126] However, he considers the visible change in Israeli society – in which the majority of citizens identify themselves as Jews before Israeli – as highly problematic for the continuation of the integration process of minority groups. Later research by Munayer – conducted in 2014 – seems to confirm this sombre prediction. Arab Christians no longer view the Jewish nation "as a model of, and a vehicle to, Western culture and values" due to the rise of religious nationalism in Israeli society.[127]

Munayer's field study provides helpful insight into some of the societal pressures faced by Palestinian Arab Christians in Israel. Although it is unclear if – and to what extent – the findings can be applied to the target group of this comparative study, it is reasonable to assume that Arab Evangelical also encounter some of the same issues uncovered in this research project. Nevertheless, their close connection to the evangelical community around the world – since the nineteenth and twentieth century – might be a reason to question the notion that they viewed the Jewish state as a vehicle to Westernisation.

4.2.3 The Collective Identity of Arab Baptist Leaders in the Holy Land

The first and, thus far, only qualitative research project on identity formation of Arab Evangelicals in Israel has been conducted by Ajaj and Miller.[128] Even though it is limited in scope – the interviews are only conducted with Baptist leaders – it provides a first insight into some of the issues faced by believers of evangelical faith in the Holy Land. The primary focus of their research was "to explore the collective identity of Arab Baptists in Israel".[129] The model used for their project is based on Green's

---

[126]   Munayer suggests that the process of Westernisation among Arab Christians finds its origin in the education provided by church denominations from the West in the nineteenth and twentieth century. Munayer, 117.

[127]   This view assumes a correlation between the rise of religious nationalism and a growing detachment from the West. However, the author of this thesis would like to point out that the strong friendship between President Trump and Prime Minister Netanyahu and the strengthening of the bond between both countries might suggest the opposite. Salim J. Munayer and Gabriel Horenczyk, 'Multi-Group Acculturation Orientations in a Changing Context: Palestinian Christian Arab Adolescents in Israel after the Lost Decade', *International Journal of Psychology* 49, no. 5 (October 2014): 368.

[128]   Ajaj, Miller, and Sumpter, *Arab Evangelicals in Israel*, 52–64.

[129]   Ajaj, Miller, and Sumpter, 52.

research among Muslim-background believers in South Asia.[130] This missiological scholar makes the distinction between three layers of identity –
i.e. core, social and corporate – in which the third layer is "often formulated in terms of affinity/opposition to other communities."[131] Even
though the findings of their research project cannot be generalised– due
to the limited scope of the sample group – they offer a number of interesting insights.

The Baptist leaders stated in the interviews that they prefer to identify
themselves, first and foremost, by their religion (Christian) before their
ethnicity (Arab/Palestinian) or nationality (Israeli). One of the participants acknowledged that there has been a noticeable change from forty
years ago when their Arab identity was more prominent than their religious beliefs and affiliation.[132] Possibly, as result, Baptist leaders have become – predominantly – agnostic towards Israeli politics.[133]

Another interesting finding to emerge from the interviews is the
change of attitudes by Baptist leaders towards ecumenical dialogue. Ajaj
and Miller point out that "thirty or forty years ago almost all Baptists had
recently converted from these forms of Christianity" and, for this reason,
their view of these church denominations had been very negative.[134]
Therefore, there were not eager to be in contact with them beyond the
opportunity to witness about their newly-found faith. However, nowadays, Baptists seem to define themselves less by what they are not (nominal Christians) but more by who they are (Evangelicals). This change of
perspective has opened the door for a renewed dialogue between members
of these church denominations. Nonetheless, the interviewees were not in
favour of intermarriages between nominal and evangelical Christians
while, at the same time, they had no objections towards Baptists marrying
Messianic Jews, Muslim-background believers or Arab Evangelicals from
another Protestant denominations. Therefore, Ajaj and Miller carefully

---

[130] This model will be explained in more detail in §4.3.1. Tim Green, 'Identity Issues
       for Ex-Muslim Christians, with Particular Reference to Marriage', *St Francis Maga-
       zine* 8, no. 4 (2012): 435–81.
[131] Ajaj and Miller identified four outside-groups, namely: other evangelicals, non-
       evangelical Christians, Jews and Muslims. Ajaj, Miller, and Sumpter, *Arab Evangel-
       icals in Israel*, 53.
[132] Ajaj, Miller, and Sumpter, 57.
[133] Later on, the authors point out that this attitude of Arab Evangelicals is in sharp
       contrast and conflict with Messianic Jews who consider the political develop-
       ments in Israel and the region of great importance to their faith. Ajaj, Miller, and
       Sumpter, 63, 86.
[134] Ajaj, Miller, and Sumpter, 58.

conclude that "Baptists center their identity around a particular doctrinal tradition... more than certain cultural customs."[135] Their evangelical faith seems to be the strongest boundary marker – even more so than the label 'Baptist' – in relation to other communities in the Holy Land.

This field study of Ajaj and Miller therefore, helpfully provides an initial glimpse into the identity formation of Arab Evangelicals in Israel. However, more research is required – for example, among lay people or ministers from other Evangelical denominations – in order to gain a thorough understanding of the issues faced by the members of this target group.[136]

4.3   Muslim-Background Believers

In recent decades, the topic of identity formation – especially, among Jesus followers in the House of Islam – has generated much interest in the field of missiology.[137] Academics and practitioners have discussed extensively the social, cultural and religious changes that (should) occur if a Muslim comes to faith in Christ. Missiological concerns – such as: evangelism, conversion, discipleship and church planting – seem to be, in one way or another, all related to the topic of identity formation.[138] It is beyond the scope of this thesis to provide a complete overview of the research conducted in this field of study, but the most relevant studies to this thesis will be presented and discussed.

---

[135]   Ajaj, Miller, and Sumpter, 58.

[136]   In 2015, a conference was organised on the topic of 'Palestinian Christian Identity in Israel' by Musalaha, Truman Institute, The Swiss Center of Conflict Research, The Hebrew University of Jerusalem and The Center for the Study of Christianity. No papers were published in the aftermath of the conference, but the presentations can be watched on YouTube. In relation to the topic of this thesis, the ongoing research projects of Natalie Layus and Lara Issa might be of interest in the future. 'Palestinian Christian Identity in Israel: New Trends of Research [accessed 1/11/2019]' (Jerusalem, 2015), https://www.youtube.com/user/musalahagalil/videos.

[137]   The first study on this topic was by Syrjänen in the 1980s and has laid much of the groundwork for the subsequent studies on identity formation of Muslim-background believers. Seppo Syrjänen, *In Search of Meaning and Identity: Conversion to Christianity in Pakistani Muslim Culture*, Finnish Society for Missiology and Ecumenics 45 (Helsinki: Finnish Society for Missiology and Ecumenics, 1984).

[138]   The following books on Insider Movements provide a clear illustration of this phenomenon. Ayman S. Ibrahim and Ant B. Greenham, eds., *Muslim Conversions to Christ: A Critique of Insider Movements in Islamic Contexts* (New York: Peter Lang, 2018), chaps 7–11, 14.; Talman and Travis, *Understanding Insider Movements*, chaps 58–64.

4.3.1 Spiritual Migrants

Tim Green's research on the conversion experiences of Muslim-background believers in Pakistan is one of the most frequently quoted studies on the issue of identity formation among Jesus followers in the House of Islam.[139] Based on his literature study, he presents a dynamic model with three layers of identity (Figure 1) in which *core* refers to the construction of a personal identity, *social* to the formation of an individual identity within a community, and *corporate* to the positioning of a group within society. Green used this identity framework to conduct thirty-two interviews among first-generation believers in Pakistan.

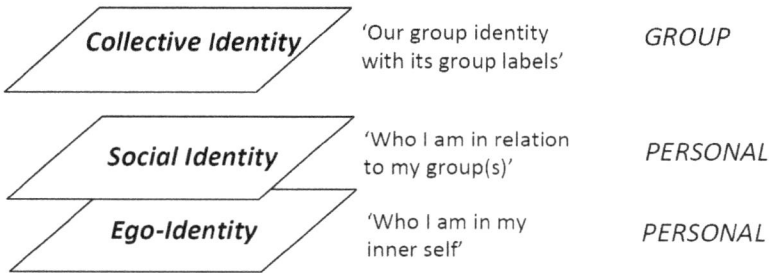

Collective Identity	'Our group identity with its group labels'	*GROUP*
Social Identity	'Who I am in relation to my group(s)'	*PERSONAL*
Ego-Identity	'Who I am in my inner self'	*PERSONAL*

Figure 1: Identity at Three Levels by Tim Green[140]

From the results of his qualitative research, Green compares the experiences of these Jesus followers with migrants because they:

> have made the journey from one faith another. They, too, undergo deep loss and change, especially when family is left behind. They, too, have to find a new community, learn its "language" and unwritten codes of conduct. They, too, struggle with integrating their old and new identities and wonder how many it will take before they truly feel at home.[141]

---

[139]   Tim Green, 'Issues of Identity for Christians of a Muslim Background in Pakistan' (London, University of London, 2014).
[140]   Green, 26.
[141]   Tim Green, 'Conversion in the Light of Identity Theories', in *Longing for Community: Church, Ummah, or Somewhere in Between?*, ed. David Greenlee (Pasadena, CA: William Carey Library, 2013), 41.

Subsequently, these 'spiritual migrants' find themselves on the border-zone of Islam and Christianity and are confronted with a sense of dual-belonging to both religious communities. Based on his research, Green observes that Muslim-background believers in Pakistan find it increasingly difficult to live in this tension, especially when they get married and raise children.[142] In his interviews, the participants describe in detail the problems they encounter on each level – core, social and corporate – of their identity. Green observes various coping strategies among these Jesus followers, such as: 1) switching between both religious communities until they are forced to choose between one of them; 2) supressing one side of their social identity by associating completely with the other religious community; 3) finding a synthesis – through the creation of a "third culture" – which is tolerated by their family members and friends.[143] Green recognises that the third option is nearly impossible for first-generation believers but, at the same time, claims that it is the most sustainable solution for them. Therefore, he is in favour of Muslim-background believers forming a (temporary) hybrid identity in order that the second-generation Jesus followers will be able – as their numbers grow – to create a new collective identity in Islamic societies.

Kathryn Kraft arrives at a similar conclusion in her sociological study on Muslim-background believers in Lebanon and Egypt.[144] Even though her research mainly focusses on the influence of Islamic doctrine and Arab values – such as, "unity" and "shame and honour" – when it concerns the identity formation of these Jesus followers, she also concludes that:

> The participants who demonstrated the greatest degree of comfort with a well-developed identity were those who had successfully adhered a Christian religious identity onto a pre-existing Muslim ethnic identity.[145]

Nevertheless, she also acknowledges that Muslim-background believers (re-)negotiate their religious identity differently:

> Some reject everything about their past and choose to become fully "Christian". These are the individuals who are most likely to break off relations

---

[142] Green, 'Issues of Identity for Christians of a Muslim Background in Pakistan', 291.
[143] Tim Green, 'Identity Choices at the Border Zone', in *Longing for Community: Church, Ummah, or Somewhere in Between?*, ed. David Greenlee (Pasadena, CA: William Carey Library, 2013), 56–57.
[144] Kathryn Ann Kraft, 'Community and Identity among Arabs of a Muslim Background Who Choose to Follow a Christian Faith' (Bristol, University of Bristol, 2007).
[145] Kraft, 213.

with their former communities. Others consider their faith and their ethnicity to be completely separate and consider themselves to be both Muslim and followers of Christ; some of these sought to be socially indistinguishable from their Muslim neighbours.[146]

Based on these observations, Kraft's research seems to confirm the notion that forming a hybrid identity is difficult – perhaps impossible – for first-generation Jesus followers but, at the same time, the most sustainable solution for them.[147]

The complexity of multiple belonging and hybrid identification becomes even more visible in a study by Jens Barnett.[148] Based on his literature review and a number of in-depth interviews with Muslim-background believers in the Levant region, he argues that the one-dimensional paradigms – such as, the C-scale of Travis – are too simplistic and, therefore, inadequate.[149] He proposes a dialogical paradigm in which culture(s), worldview(s), belonging(s) and role(s); each have a voice in the dynamic conversation of the *self*. In this way, the personal and changing nature of identity formation – as visualised by Barnett in Figure 2 – becomes evident and, as such, the model provides a helpful insight into the complexity of multiple belonging and hybrid identification among Muslim-background believers in the Levant.[150]

---

[146] Kraft, 213.

[147] Hence, Green and Kraft are more concerned about the *consequences* of conversion – especially with regards to identity formation – than the *reasons* for or *processes* of this change in faith and/or religious affiliation. Green, 'Issues of Identity for Christians of a Muslim Background in Pakistan', 292.; Kraft, 'Community and Identity among Arabs of a Muslim Background Who Choose to Follow a Christian Faith', 215.

[148] Barnett, 'Conversion's Consequences: Identity, Belonging, and Hybridity amongst Muslim Followers of Christ [Unpublished Thesis]'.

[149] Barnett, 22–26, 86.

[150] Barnett notes, by the way, that the interviewees already had hyphenated identities and experienced multiple religio-cultural belonging before they came to faith in Jesus – although they might have not been aware of it – because it is part of modern life in an increasingly globalised and pluralistic world. Jens Barnett, 'Refusing to Choose: Multiple Belonging among Arab Followers of Christ', in *Longing for Community: Church, Ummah, or Somewhere in Between?*, ed. David Greenlee (Pasadena, CA: William Carey Library, 2013), 28.

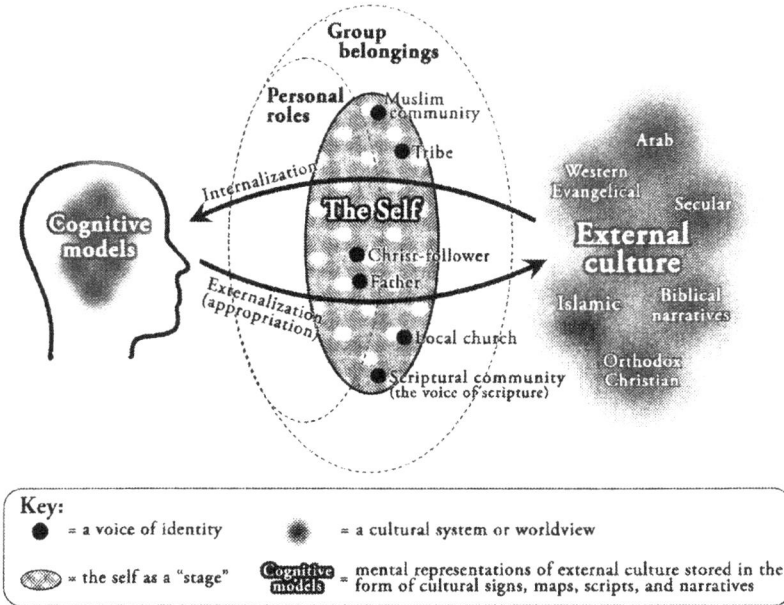

Figure 2: The Dialogical Paradigm by Jens Barnett[151]

As previously stated, researchers are not only concerned with describing the identity formation of Muslim-background believers but also finding out the most effective way of (re-)negotiating a new identity. Scholars from the field of missiology especially, discuss this issue in great detail. These debates and models do not remain theoretical, but are often experimented with as they are put into practice. Consequently, this gives rise to a number of questions such as: how should these Jesus followers raise their children? Which national and religious holidays can they continue to observe? Should they become part of an Evangelical church or can they stay within their community and religion of birth as members of an *Insider Movement*? Are there benefits to changing their religious status legally?

With regard to these kinds of questions, Greenlee provides a number of interesting insights in his article *Living Out an "In Christ" Identity*.[152]

---

[151] Barnett, 27.

[152] David Greenlee, 'Living Out an "In Christ" Identity: Research and Reflections Related to Muslims Who Have Come to Faith in Jesus Christ', *International Journal of Frontier Missiology* 30, no. 1 (2013): 5–12.

Based on the research of Green, Kraft and Barnett, he argues that identity formation should be seen as a dynamic process in which there are levels of continuity and discontinuity. Muslim-background believers may experience no changes – for example – in the way they wash their hands or the food they like to eat. The same might be true for most of their preferences with regards to their social, cultural, national and religious backgrounds. However, Greenlee argues that "the question of believing [in Jesus], or not believing, is the core discontinuity between those are who are "in Christ" and those who are not."[153] Furthermore, he regards the authority of Scripture, biblical understanding of grace and submission to God as core issues of discontinuity. Interestingly, as discussed in §1.5, these criteria can be considered boundary markers of Evangelicalism – especially, the focus on *beliefs* rather than *religious practices* – but are by no means universally accepted by the Church. Does this imply that being "in Christ" is the same as identifying as an evangelical? Greenlee concludes his essay by arguing that "We celebrate our diversity, but remember that it is not of an undefined variety. Our identity – whatever its outward expression – is given, grounded and deeply rooted in Christ."[154]

Thus far, the studies discussed have provided a number of meaningful insights into the dynamic process of identity formation – which can be compared with 'spiritual migration' or a 'conversation with multiple narratives' – of Muslim-background believers. However, this raises the question of whether these findings relate to the experiences of Muslim-background believers in Israel.

4.3.2 Evangelism and Conversion in the Holy Land

Since the turn of the millennium, two field studies have been conducted among members of the target group.[155] Although these research projects were not primarily focussed on *identity formation*, the topics were closely related – namely, *conversion* and *evangelism* – and investigated from the field of missiology.

---

[153] Greenlee, 10.
[154] Greenlee, 11.
[155] The author is aware of one more field study conducted in the Holy Land, but the findings of this research project could not be used for this thesis as it would expose – against the expressed wishes of the researcher – the location of the field study. Through his personal contact with the researcher, the author became aware of the geographically area of this field study but the report itself uses pseudonyms only.

In 2003, Ant Greenham interviewed twenty-two Muslim-background believers in the Holy Land. Based on his findings, he concludes that there are five factors which play an important role in their conversion – namely, the person of Jesus, Bible reading, the role of other believers, the truth of the gospel and God's involvement through the miraculous.[156] According to Greenham, "other findings [from field studies] clarify and confirm these results and suggest they apply broadly to other Muslim converts also."[157] Miller proposes that these factors are still key, to a large extent, for Muslims coming to faith within the Holy Land.[158]

One of the interesting insights from Greenham's field study is that the interviewees indicated that they were not committed to or involved in Islam before their conversion.[159] Therefore, they do not claim that they had rejected their religion of birth but, rather, started to pursue God after they encountered the person of Jesus.[160] With regards to identity formation, this is an interesting finding because it suggests that the interviewees did not only change their religious affiliation but also became (more) religious because of their conversion.

Greenham's field study also seems to suggest that communal factors play an important role in Palestinian Muslim women coming to faith within the Holy Land.[161] Although further research is required to confirm this finding, it is an interesting observation with regards to identity formation. It raises a number of questions, mainly around the significance of a personal encounter with Christ for (re-)negotiating one's identity and whether women have the same conversation with the *self* – to use Barnett's terminology – as men if they have come to faith through a communal decision rather than a personal choice. Also, the question could be asked if these women form a different core, social and corporate identities – in

---

[156] Greenham, 'Muslim Conversions to Christ: An Investigation of Palestinian Converts Living in the Holy Land', 197–215.

[157] Greenham, 230.

[158] Ajaj, Miller, and Sumpter, *Arab Evangelicals in Israel*, 102.

[159] Greenham, 'Muslim Conversions to Christ: An Investigation of Palestinian Converts Living in the Holy Land', 233.

[160] From Dunning's field study a different picture emerges, namely that Muslim-background believers in the West Bank are very critical towards and negative about Islam. Dunning, 'Palestinian Muslims Converting to Christianity: Effective Evangelistic Methods in the West Bank.', 212.

[161] Even though it is not clear what Greenham means with the word "communal", it is – within a patriarchal society – not uncommon for Muslim women to follow their husbands after they have come to faith in Jesus. Greenham, 'Muslim Conversions to Christ: An Investigation of Palestinian Converts Living in the Holy Land', 234–35.

accordance with Green's model – than men. Ultimately, this observation queries whether the identity paradigms – as presented above – take into account the differences in personal and communal decision-making processes.

In 2014, Craig Dunning conducted a field study project on effective methods of evangelism in the West Bank.[162] Although his research is mainly focussed on the stages *before* and *during* rather than *after* conversion, he presents a number of interesting findings on the identity formation of Muslim-background believers in the Holy Land.[163]

Describing the culture of the West Bank, Dunning suggests that Palestinian Arab identity is mainly formed by "[the] primary use of the Arabic language, a shared historical identity, as well as common values and traditions."[164] Furthermore, the 'honour-shame' worldview and Palestinian nationalism binds them together as a people group within the Greater Arab Family. Interestingly, based on the results of twenty-four interviews, Dunning observes that Muslim-background believers in the West Bank "do not consider the issue of Palestine to be as important as the gospel".[165] Because, they believe that "true social change occurs only as a result of spiritual change."[166] This observation seems to suggest that politics became less important to the interviewees after their conversion.

With regards to church affiliation, most of the participants said they were in some way connected to a community of evangelical faith.[167] Unfortunately, it is unclear whether they were referring to traditional or evangelical churches even though most of them indicated that they gather on a Friday or a Saturday. Arguably, meeting on those weekend days in Islamic society raises less suspicion in their community of birth. With regards to religious rituals, half of the interviewees said that they had been baptised. Most of them picked a place outdoors rather than in a church

---

[162] Even though the field research was not conducted in Israel proper, some of the findings are still highly relevant for the research topic of this thesis. Dunning, 'Palestinian Muslims Converting to Christianity: Effective Evangelistic Methods in the West Bank.'

[163] In chapter 3, Dunning discusses briefly the issue of self-identity in relation to contextualisation, evangelism and post-conversion. However, he is more concerned about clarifying some theological and missiological matters rather than exploring the identity formation of Muslim-background believers. Dunning, 129–38.

[164] Dunning, 68.

[165] However, one would be mistaken to assume that the interviewees are politically neutral with regards to the Israeli occupation or the creation of a Palestinian State. Dunning, 289.

[166] Dunning, 290.

[167] Dunning, 289.

building. Most likely, safety concerns were the main reason for this decision. With regards to the process of identity formation, it would be interesting to investigate the reasons for and consequences of this 'loose' affiliation with local churches; especially, whether these Jesus followers remain connected to their community of evangelical faith or not and, subsequently, how this affects their newly-found faith long-term.

In conclusion, it has become clear that there are a significant number of studies on the identity formation of Muslim-background believers in the House of Islam but that there is only limited data available on the experiences of these Jesus followers in the Holy Land. The same could be said about the other two target groups. Thus, questions emerge around which models, concepts and themes can be used to conduct a comparative study.

5: Missiological Framework for a Comparative Study

The literature review has provided an indication of the historical, cultural, sociological and theological factors at play in the identity formation of Messianic Jews, Arab Evangelicals and Muslim-background believers in Israel. However, it is important to question how their experiences – which are often multi-layered and difficult to fully comprehend – can be compared. In this chapter, a missiological framework for a comparative study will be presented based on the findings of the literature review.

5.1 Missiological Perspective

The primary objective of this research project is to describe, analyse and compare the identity formation of believers of evangelical faith in Israel. As already indicated in the introduction, the research question can be investigated from various fields of study. Any research project on this topic needs, therefore, to take into consideration the breadth of data available. However, the complexity of the research topic also requires a certain level of depth. Hence, the concepts and themes selected from the literature review are, first and foremost, related to the field of missiology.

Notably, themes of topics of conversion and identity formation are closely associated in the literature – especially in the field of religious studies and missiology – but they are not exactly the same subject matter.[168] As already pointed out in §4.3.1, conversion is related to the *factors* and *processes* of change in faith and/or religious affiliation whereas identity formation is more concerned about the *consequences* of these occurrences. This is an important distinction to make, because they refer to different stages of the faith journey. Within the field of missiology, it could be argued that conversion is more related to the topic of evangelism and identity formation to the subject of discipleship. From an evangelical perspective, the first refers to the start of someone's faith journey while the second one is a life-long journey of faith. Even though these religious experiences cannot be separated, they are not referring to the same events or processes either. Therefore, the missiological framework for a comparative study presented in this chapter is concerned with the identity formation of a Jesus follower *after* he or she has come to faith in Christ.

---

[168] Miller, *Living among the Breakage*, 70.

5.2   Key Concepts

From the literature review, Warshawsky's notion of 'identity-as-travel' and Green's concept of 'spiritual migrants' seem to provide common ground to describe and compare the identity formation of Messianic Jews and Muslim-background believers. The terminology used by these researchers includes a number of significant concepts – namely: roots and routes, boundary crossing and boundary marking, newness and renewal, dual-belonging and hybrid identity, and so forth – and is echoed by other scholars in the field. Therefore, the research of Warshawsky and Green will be used as a foundation for the missiological framework for a comparative study as presented in this chapter.

Green's dynamic model which presents three layers of identity – namely; core, social and corporate – is frequently used in field studies conducted among Muslim-background believers in the House of Islam. In addition, the literature review has demonstrated that it can also be easily adapted for research projects in other geographical and religious settings, such as: Ajaj and Miller's field study on the collective identity of Arab Baptist leaders in Israel. The simplicity of the model allows for a meaningful conversation between various fields of study. Therefore, it will be used as a blueprint for comparing the identity formation of believers of evangelical faith in Israel.

5.3   Themes

There are a number of themes that have emerged from the literature review which are of key interest to the field of missiology.

Firstly, in which aspects of their lives do believers of evangelical faith in Israel experience *discontinuity* as a direct result of their conversion? And, alternatively, in which areas do they encounter *continuity* after they have come to faith in Jesus? Subsequently, what is the reason behind these differences? Are they related to their core, social and/or corporate identities? What is the influence of their community of birth and the impact of their community of evangelical faith with regards to the level of (dis)continuity? What seems to be the most fruitful and sustainable solution for their identity formation as Jesus followers from a Jewish, Muslim or Christian background?

Secondly, do members of the target group seek a *new* or *renewed* identity? Or, with the words of Warshawsky, *newness* or *renewal*? And, to what extent, is this a result of their worldview and/or the influence of foreign mission workers? How does this effect the way in which they view their religion of birth? What are the implications for discipleship among these Jesus followers?

Thirdly, to what extent do the members of these communities of evangelical faith in Israel form their core, social and corporate identities in a *similar* way? And, if so, is this directly related to their historical connection with evangelical Protestantism or are there other factors at play? What is the influence of their common language(s), culture, worldview, country of residence, minority status? Could fruitful practices be adopted by members of the other target groups because of these *similarities*?

In conclusion, based on the key concepts and themes mentioned above, the author of this thesis proposes a missiological framework for a comparative study between Messianic Jews, Arab Evangelicals and Muslim-background believers in Israel which incorporates these main elements. Together, they form the basis of the central research question and sub-questions, as presented in §1.3, and serve as a foundation for the field study.

6: Methodology

A field study was conducted among members of the target groups in order to fill the gaps within the literature and to generate new data for a comparative study between Messianic Jews, Arab Evangelicals and Muslim-background believers in Israel. This chapter will provide an account of the research process and the methodology used.

6.1 Data Collection

Nine *semi-structured interviews* were conducted with believers of evangelical faith in the north of Israel during the fall of 2019. With the assistance of *gatekeepers*, the researcher found a sufficient number of participants who met the criteria of the field study.[169] The *size of the sample group* was determined – i.e. three members of each target group – by the researcher and his thesis advisor beforehand.

To secure the safety and anonymity of the interviewees, their names were shortened to a number with an abbreviation of their community of evangelical faith for this thesis. In addition, the personal details listed in Figure 3 and described in the findings of the field study are reduced to a bare minimum. In accordance with the ETF Checklist Ethical Acceptability, the consent of the participants was asked beforehand and they could withdraw from the interview at any time. Furthermore, the recordings and notes of the interviews will be deleted after this master's thesis is submitted and graded.

---

[169] The following criteria were communicated to the gatekeepers: the participants 1) have experienced some form of change or transformation from their religion of birth to faith in Jesus; 2) were born and raised in Israel; 3) live in the north of Israel (close to Haifa or Nazareth); 4) do not know the researcher personally; 5) have the ability to express themselves in English; 6) are from a Muslim, Jewish or nominal Christian background; 7) attend an Evangelical church, Messianic congregation or Christian fellowship.

#	Name	Sex	Age	Status	Children	Age at Coming to Faith	Age at Baptism
1	AE1	Female	±55	Married	1	±27	±29
2	AE2	Female	±35	Married	0	±31	±25
3	MJ1	Female	±45	Divorced	3	±12	±17
4	AE3	Male	±40	Married	3	±26	±28
5	MBB1	Female	±38	Married	3	±24	±26
6	MBB2	Male	±50	Single	0	±18	±23
7	MBB3	Female	±25	Relation-ship	0	±23	±25
8	MJ2	Male	±35	Married	0	±31	±32
9	MJ3	Female	±65	Married	3	±19	±21

Figure 3: Personal Details of the Participants in the Field Study

Eight out of nine interviews were conducted in English. Only one inter-viewee (AE3) was not able to answer the questions in this language, but his wife (MBB1) translated for him. The researcher's ability to converse in He-brew and – to a lesser extent – in Arabic, proved to be a major asset in this field study. Participants felt comfortable to use terminology from their own languages when it became difficult to answer some of the more per-sonal questions in their second or third language. Furthermore, the re-searcher's interest in the target groups was immediately shown by his abil-ity to converse in these languages even though – as will be discussed in §6.2 and §9.3 – this was not without difficulties. To avoid any confusion, the researcher clarified his close connection to the communities of evan-gelical faith in Israel before each interview.

The semi-structured interviews lasted, on average, an hour. The conver-sations were *recorded* and, simultaneously, *notes* were taken by an independ-ent observer. Based on this data, the researcher wrote a *summary report* of each interview – using the personal pronoun in order to stay as close as pos-sible to the original text – and confirmed the accuracy with every participant. For the sake of clarity, the researcher has occasionally added a word or term in brackets to ensure that the meaning of a sentence is understood by the reader. For privacy and safety reasons, the interview summary reports have not been added to the appendix but they are available upon request.

The presence of a third person in the room – namely, the wife of the interviewer who took notes during the conversations – resulted in more openness among the female interviewees. Most likely, they would not have felt as comfortable to share their personal thoughts and feelings with a male researcher if she had not been present. Although, this issue was not foreseen, upon reflection, it proved to be a very useful to the interviewees and interviewer.

The questions asked during the interviews were derived from the interview guides of Green and Warshawsky.[170] Only a limited number of topics was selected from these interview guides – such as: background, conversion experience, rituals and routines, terminology – which are directly related to the central research question and sub-questions of this thesis. Furthermore, the diagrams used in the interview guide of Green were adjusted to three groups – i.e. Jewish, Christian and Muslim.[171] In this way, the data generated through the field study could be visualised – as will be demonstrated in §8.1.3. Due to the fact that the research of these two scholars serves as a blueprint of the missiological framework for a comparative study between members of the target groups, as presented in chapter 5, the findings of this field study can be compared with the results of their research. Furthermore, by using their interview guides as a model – which have demonstrated their academic validity and reliability – the quality of the data generated in the field study increased significantly.

The *interview guide* of the field study was tested in a pilot project and, subsequently, re-adjusted.[172] It became apparent, for example, that the questions were too long and detailed and, as a result, led to an unnatural flow in the interviews. Subsequently, the revised version of the interview guide was compared with the questions asked in the field study of Ajaj & Miller.[173] Which resulted in the final version of the interview guide – see appendix 1 – being used in the field study conducted in the fall of 2019. Although not every question was asked directly by the researcher, the majority of them were answered indirectly by the interviewees during the course of the interview.

---

[170] Green, 'Issues of Identity for Christians of a Muslim Background in Pakistan', 314–20.; Warshawsky, 'Returning To Their Own Borders; A Social Anthropological Study of Contemporary Messianic Jewish Identity in Israel', 247–48.

[171] A copy of these modified diagrams can be found in the interview guide in the appendix.

[172] The results of the pilot project conducted among Muslim-background believers in Belgium will be presented in §6.3.

[173] Ajaj, Miller, and Sumpter, *Arab Evangelicals in Israel*, 54.

In conclusion, Verhoeven points out that conducting qualitative research requires an attitude of continuous reflection on the process and, if necessary, a readiness to change the procedure.[174] As such, doing research should be understood as an *iterative process*. This principle was applied throughout the field study as demonstrated above. Numerous changes were made to the original research proposal – based on the feedback received from the professors, classmates and participants of the pilot project – in order to improve the quality of the data generated by this field study.

6.2 Limitations

During the field study, a number of limitations emerged which need to be acknowledged.

Firstly, the researcher's close ties with the communities of evangelical faith in the north of Israel meant that the number of suitable candidates for the interviews was limited – to secure the reliability of the data obtained, he was advised by his supervisor not to interview anyone he knows personally. However, with the assistance of local gatekeepers, nine believers were found – three from each target group – who wanted to participate in the field study.

Secondly, the researcher could only stay in the north of Israel for ten days and, therefore, was working under time constraints. Before arriving in Israel, he had only been able to arrange one interview. However, once he had arrived, the gatekeepers proved to be very helpful in securing enough participants for his research project.

Thirdly, during the initial stages of the field study, the researcher wondered if he should extend the geographical area of the target groups in order to find more suitable candidates for his field study. However, based on his literature review, he realised that this would increase the variables of the data generated significantly because of the political tension and religious conflict in other parts of the country. Believers of evangelical faith in Jerusalem and the West Bank go through radically different experiences than those in the north of Israel. In cities like Haifa and Nazareth, religious and ethnic communities live more peacefully and harmoniously with one another than in other cities in the Holy Land. To his relief, the researcher was able to access, in the end, enough participants for his field study in the north of Israel.

---

[174] Pieternella Susanna Verhoeven, *Doing research: the hows and whys of applied research* (Chicago: Lyceum Books, 2008), 151.

Fourthly, as already mentioned, one of the interviewees (AE2) was not able to conduct the interview in English. Fortunately, his wife (MBB1) – who was also being interviewed – offered to translate for him. Also, the level of English of MBB3 seemed to be quite limited in the communication leading up to the interview. She had suggested to bring her boyfriend alongside her, but he cancelled at the last minute. However, in the end, her English proved to be good enough the conduct an in-depth interview.

Fifthly, a number of the interviewees used Hebrew or Arabic words in describing their experiences. Although the researcher was familiar with most of the terms used, on a number of occasions he had to ask for clarification during the conversation or find the correct translation afterwards when listening to the recordings and summarising the interviews.

Sixthly, it became evident during the interviews that some of the questions listed on the interview guide could not be asked because they were too personal or sensitive. For example, a number of the participants were not married and/or did not have children. For this reason, question 23 of the interview guide was not always asked if it was considered inappropriate. Similarly, it became clear that question 16.1 of the interview guide was not always appreciated by the participants because it touched on a sensitive topic with regards to their nationality. Due to the fact that it was not the primary objective of this field study to describe the political views and affiliation of the participants, this question was sometimes left out of the interview.

Seventhly, the imbalance in the male-female ratio of interviewees (3/6) was only noticed after the field study was completed. Although this might have affected the data collected, the researcher is confident that the impact on the outcomes of this research project is limited.

Eighthly, the literature review already indicated a close connection between 'conversion' and 'identity formation'. This also became evident in the field study and, as a result, it was not possible to disconnect these topics when writing up the findings. However, the discussion in chapter 8 will focus only on the identity formation of members of the target groups in order to be able to answer the central research question and sub-questions.

Finally, it should be pointed out that a close connection between a researcher and a target group is not without difficulties – as already mentioned in §1.6. The most commonly cited objection towards, for example, ethnographic research is that the observation of the 'other' becomes tainted and, thereby, less objective. To gain a greater understanding into some of the issues at play, the researcher consulted the methodology of other field studies related to the topic of this thesis. Kraft, for instance, provides a detailed account of some of the issues she encountered as somewhat of an 'insider' in her own fieldwork among Muslim-background believers in Egypt and Lebanon.[175] Even though she recognises that it is "a nearly impossible endeavour for the outsider to become native in the first place", her ability to converse in Arabic and to participate in church meetings gave her access to a community which would otherwise remain closed for academic research.[176] At the same time, her primary position as an 'outsider' – i.e. a social-science researcher from the UK – was also beneficial. During her field work, she realised that the interviewees opened up more towards her than they would have done to an 'indigenous researcher' – i.e. Arab Christian or a Muslim-background believer – because of her detachment to their communities of birth. For this reason, Kraft concludes that "defining researchers as insiders or as outsiders is largely a futile endeavour and, therefore, researching the 'other' also draws an unnecessary artificial line between researcher and researched."[177] She suggests that, ultimately, the level of reflexivity – regardless whether the researcher is a so-called 'insider' or 'outsider' – is key to the quality of data collected and analysed in a field study. With this in mind, the author has conducted his research project among members of the target groups and he will reflect on his level of reflexivity in §9.3.

6.3   Pilot Project

As already noted, a pilot project was conducted among Muslim-background believers in Belgium in the spring of 2019.[178] The objectives of this field study were, first of all, to test the interview guide and, secondly, to practice the research skills of the author. Secondly, a further aim of the project was to generate more data on the identity formation of Muslim-background believers in the West. Surprisingly, to date, limited research has been done among these Jesus followers in Europe and North America.[179]

---

[175]   Kraft, 'Community and Identity among Arabs of a Muslim Background Who Choose to Follow a Christian Faith', 67–75.

[176]   Kraft, 68.

[177]   Kraft, 69.

[178]   The pilot project was conducted in partial fulfilment of a master's course called "Field Study Project". Peter Lawrence, 'Muslim-Background Believers in Belgium in Search of a Renewed Identity as Followers of Jesus, an Enquiry [Unpublished Field Study Project]' (ETF, Leuven, 2019).

[179]   Only two missiological studies could be found, namely on the experiences of Muslim-background believers from Iran who live in the diaspora: Miller, *Living among the Breakage*, 175–204.; Roy Oksnevad, 'BMB Discipleship: An Investigation into the

During the pilot project, the question emerged whether open-ended narrative interviews might generate more valuable data than the more commonly used semi-structured interviews. This interview type was, for example, selected by Kraft in her field study on identity formation among Muslim-background believers in Lebanon and Egypt.[180] The author discussed the benefits and drawbacks of this interview type with Kraft during a personal conversation in November 2018. The main reason for choosing to conduct semi-structured interviews was based on the argument that the findings of the pilot project could be more easily compared with the results of other field studies, most notably Green's and Warshawsky's research. Although the research project among Muslim-background believers in Belgium demonstrated the limitations of this interview type – namely, the participants were more focussed on answering the questions of the interview guide than narrating their faith journey – it became clear that the data generated was rich and structured and, as such, provided a meaningful contribution to this emerging field of study. Therefore, this interview type was also used in the field study of this thesis. However, a number of changes were made to the interview guide – as already discussed in §6.1 – and the researcher made a conscious effort to listen to the narratives of the interviewees without asking any question during the first twenty minutes of the conversation.[181] In this way, he tried to combine the positive elements of both interview types in the field study of his thesis.

The findings of the field study project demonstrated that the interviewees form their identity on evangelical beliefs and practices even though they do not identify themselves as evangelicals. Their sense of belonging is with their local church rather than the global church. Therefore, by leaving the House of Islam, they have not only lost their religion of birth but also their community of birth. From their perspective, the first is replaced by faith in Jesus but the second one leaves a big void. Subsequently, the interviewees experience a profound sense of loneliness. This is one example of some of the major changes they have encountered in their core, social and corporate identities after they came to faith in Jesus. The levels of discontinuity are also seen in the terminology they use, the rituals they practice, and the freedom they experience. However, the interviewees also

---

Factors Leading to Disharmony within the Iranian Churches in the Diaspora', *St Francis Magazine* 8, no. 4 (2012): 397–434.

[180] Kraft, 'Community and Identity among Arabs of a Muslim Background Who Choose to Follow a Christian Faith', 46–56.

[181] The first question of each interview was as follows: "Can you tell me something about your background and how you came to faith in Jesus?"

indicated that there are levels of continuity after they came to faith especially with regards to their culture, ethnicity and nationality. Some of them even pointed out that their newly-found faith enhances rather than hinders these aspects of their identity. More findings could be presented, but these are the key themes to emerge from the pilot project. Although the sample group was too small in order to generalise the results, it provided a glimpse into the identity formation of Muslim-background believers in Belgium.

Based on the feedback of the professors and his fellow students, the researcher became aware that the central research question and sub-questions of the field study project were, at times, too normative and suggestive, as a result, the terminology was changed and the focus of the inquiry readjusted.[182] These modifications had also a profound effect on the research proposal of this master's thesis. Furthermore, it became evident that one of the sub-questions of the pilot project could not be answered through the research methodology selected and was, subsequently, omitted from the master's thesis.[183] Overall, the planning and execution of the field study project in Belgium proved to be an invaluable experience in preparing and conducting the semi-structured interviews in the north of Israel.

6.4   Guidelines for Data Analysis

The findings of the field study will be analysed in the following chapter based on the guidelines of Bryman.[184] He proposes that researchers need to detect from the data collected; repetitions, transitions, indigenous typologies and categories, similarities and differences, linguistic connectors, missing data – that which has not been said in the interviews – and theory-related material. This kind of data analysis can be achieved by: 1) coding the various themes

---

[182]   For example, the initial research question of the field study project was stated as follows "How do Muslim-background believers in Belgium form a (re)new(ed) identity as followers of Jesus?" Upon reflection, the author realised that this question only allows for two possible answers – namely, *new* or *renewed*. Subsequently, the central research question of this thesis was stated more broadly and open-ended.

[183]   The sub-question was stated as follows: "Do Muslim converts seek a new and/or renewed identity in Christ and, subsequently, to what extent is this an indication of their dualistic/holistic worldview?" Although the literature had indicated that there might be a possible correlation, most notably Jens Barnett, the pilot project did not generate sufficient data to investigate this notion. Jens Barnett, 'Narrative, Identity and Discipleship', *Musafir: A Bulletin of Intercultural Studies* 3, no. 2 (2009): 3–5.

[184]   Alan Bryman, *Social Research Methods*, Fifth edition (Oxford: Oxford University Press, 2016), 585–88.

that occur frequently; 2) giving them corresponding names; 3) checking possible connections between the themes; 4) giving conclusive arguments on why these themes are significant; 5) justifying the themes from the literature; and, finally, 6) providing a transparent account of the process. Based on this method of *thematic analysis*, the findings of the field study will be presented in chapter 7 and, subsequently, discussed in chapter 8.

7: Findings

In the fall of 2019, nine semi-structured interviews were conducted with three members of each target group. This chapter will provide an overview of the main themes that emerged from the data of this field study.[185]

7.1 Messianic Jews

The interviewees came to faith in Jesus during different stages of their lives; MJ1 as a teenager, MJ3 in her early twenties and MJ2 when he turned thirty-one. MJ1 and MJ3 were born and raised in a religious family and, as a result, encountered persecution after they became Jesus followers. This was not the case with MJ2, who grew up in a secular family. Each one of the interviewees has been baptised, got married to a believer (MJ1 is divorced) and regularly attend a Messianic congregation. What they also have in common is that they serve in ministry – i.e. part-time and paid – with a Christian organisation or Messianic congregation in the north of Israel. Furthermore, they have been exposed to foreigners extensively, either through marriage (MJ3), close friendships (MJ2) or residence in the US (MJ1). Two of the three interviewees (MJ1 and MJ3) have children and, thus far, they have chosen to follow in the footsteps of their parents with regards to faith in *Yeshua*.

7.1.1 Spiritual Encounters on a Faith Journey

The interviewees were introduced to the faith by friends and family members who had, somehow, a connection to the Messianic movement in Israel. During the interview, MJ1 explained how her mother became a believer in *Yeshua* and, subsequently, brought her children to congregational services on Shabbat. MJ2 had a good friend in secondary school who attended a Messianic congregation and, eventually, started to join him. MJ3 was invited to a Messianic conference by her mother – who worked at a Christian guesthouse in the north of Israel – and, after much persuasion, she decided to go.

---

[185] For security and privacy reasons, as already mentioned in §6.1, the interview summary reports are only available upon request and personal details will not be disclosed in this thesis.

During the interviews, the participants described how they had a spiritual encounter *during* or *after* one of these meetings. MJ3 recalls:

> They were teaching about *Yeshua*, but a different Jesus then what I knew from the Catholic Church with all the crosses. Is he the same person? I remember myself crying... Something was pulling me; something touched my heart.

Similarly, MJ1 recalled how she "got the call and I answered it" during a summer camp and MJ2 felt that "it just clicked" after a time of asking questions about the faith. Even though the *personal encounter* with Messianic believers was instrumental in their conversion, each one of the interviewees indicated that they came to faith in Jesus through a *spiritual encounter*.

The three members of the target group described their conversion as a *process* rather than an instant *decision*. MJ1 explained how her faith grew by attending church services and youth meetings. After four years of being a believer, she felt that "it was time to do that thing [baptism]". Similarly, the other interviewees did not go through the immersion ritual immediately but waited seven months (MJ2) and two years (MJ3) after their spiritual encounter. In addition, some of them felt that the process had already begun before their conversion. MJ2 recalled:

> Actually, I started asking questions, starting with the ones who were furthest to me but still close (pastor of the congregation), then closer (parents of my friend who are leaders in the congregation here; they are my second parents) and closer (my best friend and my parents). I had different questions for each of them... And then asking myself and God.

This process lasted a number of years, before he came to the realisation that "I have been a believer for a while, but I was just never naming it." In a similar way, MJ3 described how she read:

> many [Christian] books about the faith, not the New Testament since I wouldn't touch it. I read the prophecies about the messiah. I was drawn to go to the congregation. For two years I would go to the synagogue in the morning, and to the congregation in the afternoon. I heard the gospel week after week. I was so much drawn by the breaking of bread.

Based on her own testimony, she was only 'saved' after two years when she prayed for the first time to "Lord *Yeshua*" on Yom Kippur. A personal commitment is needed at some point, she argued, because "there is a decision to make. You can't be in a process for 20 years, like my family, not making a decision." Overall, there seemed to be a general consensus among the interviewees that conversion entails, with the words of MJ2, "one particular moment but it was a process that led to it."

7.1.2 More Jewish, More Messianic

During the interviews, these members of the target group indicated that they consider themselves more Jewish since they have found their Messiah. For example, MJ3 stated that "I feel more Jewish than ever, I feel so complete, the gospel is key to the Bible, not tradition." This sentiment was echoed by MJ2, who identified himself as Israeli before his conversion – because "I saw Jewishness as a religious act" – but now sees himself, first and foremost, as a Jew because "that is what God gave me." MJ1 did not make this distinction between the terms *Israeli* and *Jew*, because "the land is promised to all the Jewish people, so I consider them all Israeli." Furthermore, she never calls herself a Christian, because "I am completely Jewish, believing in Jesus didn't make me lose my Jewishness." The other interviewees gave similar answers when they were asked to define the label 'Christian'. They continue to feel strongly connected to their community of birth – for example, all interviewees indicated that they value the tradition of male circumcision – regardless of the opposition they sometimes face by their kinsmen. Perhaps not surprisingly, the interviewees placed themselves in the Jewish circle (B) of Diagram 1.[186]

With regards to the festivals, the interviewees said that they – by and large – only observe the biblical and national holidays. In doing so, they try to stay away from the rabbinic traditions by celebrating these feasts with their families or in their messianic congregations. Only MJ3 indicated that she had returned to a synagogue, after she became a believer in Jesus, for her wedding and *bar/bat mitzvah* of her children. To the contrary, MJ2 made a conscious decision to have a civil wedding outside of the country in order to avoid having a religious wedding in Israel.[187] MJ1 responded agitatedly, when asked if she sometimes attends a synagogue, by saying "No, I am very anti-religious, especially religious Jews... I don't feel like I need to go to a synagogue. I don't feel like God is there." This sentiment towards religion – i.e. Rabbinic Judaism – was also prominent in the answers provided by MJ2. A final point of interest with regards to the

---

[186] Diagram 1 and 2 are a reference to the diagrams used in the interview guide – see appendix 1. An overview of the responses of the interviewees to the questions Q17 and Q24 will be given in §8.1.3.

[187] Jews in Israel can only get married legally by an orthodox rabbi in a religious ceremony.

festivals is that the interviewees indicated that they have no problem with Christians celebrating their own holidays, but they personally have no desire to participate in these feasts unless it is for evangelistic purposes (MJ3) or as a sign of courtesy (MJ2).

During the interviews, Messianic terminology was used frequently. The names of biblical characters were often pronounced in Hebrew rather than English. MJ3 noted, for example, that "I like to use Biblical names... Sha'ul instead of Paul." Furthermore, they refuse to pronounce the name commonly-used for Jesus in modern Hebrew – i.e. *Yeshu* – but call him by his name in ancient Hebrew, namely *Yeshua*.[188] MJ1 noted that "I would always use *Yeshua* and not Jesus" and MJ2 indicated that he even corrects people when they use the term 'Yeshu'. Similarly, the use of Christian terminology was not always appreciated during the interviews. MJ3, for example, said:

> People say to me: 'when did you converted?' You don't say that, no, no, no, you say converted? You mean: 'when I was born again and became a follower of *Yeshua*?' That is the question, not if I am a Christian because I never left my community.

The other interviewees also seemed to be sensitive towards this kind of terminology and, as already pointed out, refused to call themselves Christians. MJ2 described himself as a "Israeli Messianic Believer" and MJ1 pointed out that:

> I never call myself a Christian. I am Messianic who believes in *Yeshua* Messiah. He is the Son of God, he came to this world. He died for my sins. Theology, we are the same, I don't disagree with the Christian theology, but I would use the Jewish terminology to describe myself.

The interviewees were more hesitant when they had to position themselves in Diagram 2. In terms of community, they feel a strong connection with believers in the Christian circle although they do not want to be called Christian. Only MJ1 indicated that she has no problem with calling herself evangelical, because "most of them have the right theology". The strong bond between believers in the Jewish and Christian circle became also

---

[188]   The term 'Yeshu' is considered by some Messianic Jews a derogatory term – possibly referring to an abbreviation of the sentence 'may his name and memory be blotted out' – from the Talmudic literature. Kai Kjaer-Hansen, 'An Introduction to the Names Yehoshua/Joshua, Yeshua, Jesus and Yeshu [Accessed 24/10/2019]', 1992, https://jewsforjesus.org/answers/an-introduction-to-the-names-yehoshua/joshua-yeshua-jesus-and-yeshu/. Date accessed: 24/10/2019.

evident with regards to marriage. The interviewees regard faith in Jesus as essential in choosing a spouse regardless of their ethnic or religious background. MJ1 was the only one who said that she would find it difficult if her children were to get married to a believer who is not Jewish. In the end, all of the interviewees placed themselves in G (Diagram 2) because of the community of believers in both circles. However, they do not want to be associated with nominal Christianity and, to a lesser extent, Judaism. However, at the same time, they hold on to some of the festivals and terminology of their community of birth and re-interpreted them in light of their newly-found faith in the Messiah.

7.2   Arab Evangelicals

The three members of the target group interviewed in this field study, were born and raised in Catholic families in the north of Israel. They converted in their mid-twenties and are married to spouses who also had conversion experiences. Each of the interviewees had had an encounter with a foreigner, or someone who had lived abroad, who had turned out be instrumental in their journey towards evangelical faith. They have interacted extensively with other believers in the Holy Land, most notably Messianic Jews, but not without difficulty. The interviewees were baptised and are members of an Arab Evangelical church (AE1/AE3) and/or a Messianic congregation (AE2/AE3). Since their conversion, they have faced low levels of opposition from their friends and family members and, as a result, have been able to raise their children – AE3 has three young children and AE1 has one older daughter – within an community of evangelical faith.

7.2.1 Coming back to Church

AE1 and AE2 were introduced to the evangelical faith through the Baptist school they attended as children. Thus, from an early age, they were exposed to and part of two church denominations within Christianity. During her childhood, AE1 had a number of negative experiences with the Catholic Church and, as a result, "from that time, I had inside me something against this church. I knew there was something beyond." In a similar way, AE2 became increasingly critical of her religious and cultural background. Although she "searched for another identity" as a teenager, she continued to attend services in both church denominations during those years. This was not easy for her, and she felt constantly pressed to defend one community against the other. When she met her boyfriend, a new believer in Jesus from Argentina, she realised that "I couldn't define

myself" because she was unable to answer his question if she was catholic
or evangelical. By talking to him, AE2 also noticed that she "was getting
further and further away from God" but, at the same time, she knew that
"sometime I would get back to God." Later on, she started to attend an
Evangelical church with her boyfriend. In the same way, AE1 also experienced a longing for the evangelical faith of her youth. After a period of
searching, she was invited to a Sunday service in a Baptist church by an
American mission worker. She recalled in the interview that she danced
through the streets afterwards because "it got me back to the songs we
sang as a child." For both interviewees it was clear that the seed of evangelical faith was sown in their lives through the Baptist school they attended as children.[189]

Although each of the interviewees emphasised the importance of
church attendance in their conversion process, they also pointed out the
significance of spiritual encounters in their faith journey. They experienced healing (AE3), deliverance from demonic powers (AE2), supernatu-
ral joy (AE1), cleansing from sins (AE3), visions of Jesus (AE1, AE3), and so
forth, and were – more often than not – able to give the exact date or year
when these occurred. These spiritual encounters are also considered an
important reason by the interviewees why they had a change of mind on a
number of issues with regards to their religion of birth. AE2 explained, for
example, that:

> After the moment I was born again I was really convinced of the fact that
> you can't have Mary there... I started to understand I had to get rid of Ca-
> tholicism; the statues although I didn't have statues.

Furthermore, AE3 realised after his conversion that a personal commitment is necessary because "everyone who is born in a Christian/believing
family cannot be part of this family if he is not covered in the blood of
Jesus." Or, with the words of AE1, "to discover the love of God, to be convinced... is something you need to choose for yourself" and cannot be
based on the religious affiliation of your parents. From the answers provided, it seems that the spiritual encounters and new convictions were an
intrinsic part of their conversion process of the interviewees and are considered boundary markers of evangelical faith by these members of the
target group.

---

[189] Interestingly, both interviewees indicated that they had become less interested in
politics after their conversion and more respectful towards their culture and religion of birth.

During the interview discussions, it became clear – as already noted – that the interviewees placed a high value on church attendance. For example, AE1 and AE3 expressed their great concern for teenagers in Evangelical churches and their struggle to keep them interested in the faith. According to AE1, there is "Sunday school for kids, but when they turn 14/15 they disappear." AE3 explained that he has started a music ministry for young people because:

> There is a great need amongst young Christian Arabs, to help to put their eyes on the Lord; to support them to serve the Lord; to open a door for them to study music in a good way. Our heart is to create a place where we can teach teenagers how to play music for the Lord.

But, also, the interviewees shared about the positive influence of church attendance on their faith journeys. For example, AE2 noted:

> When you have coal, you need the fire to keep it burning. I knew this, always. When we were not in a church, I felt the need and I felt bad about it.

From the interviews, it seems that these members of the target group consider church attendance to be essential for their spiritual growth and faith endurance and, therefore, they continue to return to their Evangelical churches and Messianic congregations.

7.2.2 Being with Outsiders

Each of the interviewees – as aforementioned – had an encounter with a foreigner or someone who had lived abroad, who (re-)introduced them to the evangelical faith. AE1 was invited by an American mission worker to come a Baptist church, AE2 became interested by talking to a new convert from Argentina, and AE3 saw the radical change in the life of an old friend – with whom he was "together in many sins in the past" – who had returned from the US. These personal encounters with 'foreigners' were, more often than not, the first step in their conversion process. Although the interviewees did not mention that they have a lot of contact with believers of evangelical faith from abroad, it seemed that the invitation from an outsider was instrumental in their conversion.

During the interviews, it became apparent that these members of the target group found it difficult to define exactly who is an 'outsider' and to what extent they are considered an 'outsider' by others. One interviewee (AE1) explained that they – i.e. Arab Evangelicals – are "the minority of a minority of a minority" in Israel and another noted (AE3) that the interaction with other communities is "very complicated in our country." This sentiment was clearly felt throughout the three interviews. AE1 indicated that she finds it "easier to talk to a Catholic than to a Muslim about Jesus, because Muslims are very strict." At the same time, AE2 noted that "My society was very affected by Muslim society. We have in the culture some things that are very similar to Muslim." However, when asked where she would position herself in Diagram 2, she eventually decided that G is the closest to her everyday life as she celebrates the Jewish feasts in a Messianic congregation and the Christian festivals with her wider family. Even though AE3 practices the same holidays as AE2, he placed himself outside the circles in position D. AE1 struggled greatly with answering these questions, because she does not consider herself part of nominal Christianity (A) but at the same time is still "very much concerned with them". She sees herself somewhat part of the Messianic community, because "believers are the real children of God" but, simultaneously, feels that there is a major gap between them because "they think and believe they are above us because they are Jews, the chosen people". Although she did not indicate where she would place herself in the diagram, position A or D might arguably be the closest to her everyday experiences as an Arab Evangelical in the north of Israel. Overall, the interviewees found it easier to define who is an 'outsider' and when they are on the *outside* than who is an 'insider' and when they on the *inside*.

As mentioned before, spiritual encounters and new convictions were an intrinsic part of the testimonies they shared and these elements seemed to be, somehow, crucial in the way they identified themselves as Arab Evangelicals. However, when asked specifically in the interviews, they called themselves either 'Arab Christian' (AE3) or 'Messianic gentile' (AE2). The answer provided by AE1 demonstrates the complexity of the question asked as she noted: "I am Israeli citizen, but not Jewish. I am a Christian. I don't forget that I am Palestinian, I am Arab. I am Israeli, I am not a Palestinian citizen." This response illustrates how these members of the target group defined themselves during the interviews, namely: by *who they are not* rather than *who they are* as Arab Evangelicals.

Finally, as already pointed out, the interviewees did not mention any interaction with Evangelicals from abroad. Although, foreigners were influential during the early stages of their conversion process, they seem to be largely absent in their identity formation as believers of evangelical faith. However, the terminology used by the interviewees – such as: 'evangelical' (AE1), 'born again' (AE2), 'sinner' (AE2/AE3) – is closely connected to evangelical Protestantism. Furthermore, AE1 and AE2 indicated frequently that they find evangelism an important part of their faith and recounted a number of stories in which they shared the gospel with other Israelis in spite of their ethnic or religious background. Also, the topic of 'holiness' – which is one of the key components of the Great Awakening – emerged often in the testimonies of AE2 and AE3. For these reasons, the influence of and connection with evangelical Protestantism was clearly observable during the interviews with these members of the target group.

7.3   Muslim-Background Believers

The interviewees were born and raised in Muslim families in the north of Israel. Even though they fasted during Ramadan and sometimes wore a veil on special occasions (MBB1), they did not consider their families to be religious but rather traditional. The interviewees became interested in the evangelical faith during their late teens or early twenties. Since their conversion, they have been baptised and have become members of an Arab Evangelical church (MBB1/MBB3) and/or Messianic congregation (MBB1/MBB2). The families of MBB1 and MBB2 have accepted the newly-found faith of these two Jesus followers, although not openly and eagerly. MBB3 can be considered a 'secret believer' as she has only told her sister about her conversion. Two of the three interviewees are married to (MBB1) or in a relationship with (MBB3) an Arab Evangelical. MBB1 has three young children with AE3. MBB3 works as a teacher in a Jewish school while MBB1 and MBB2 serve with a ministry in the north of Israel. A final point that needs to be mentioned is that MBB2 did a similar field study project in the north of Israel in which he tried to find out whether and if so, how Muslim-background believers are welcomed into Evangelical churches.

7.3.1 Critical of Islam, Longing for a Pluralistic Society

During the interviews, the members of the target group described how they became very critical of their religion of birth when they were teenagers, because they saw it as the cause of conflict in the region (MBB2) or did not understand the logic behind some of the rituals (MBB1/MBB3). During the interview, MBB3 explained this experience as follows:

> Before I came to faith. I was every time in conflict with my parents. My mother wears the veil. I was always asking her "why do you wear the veil? Why you have to go to Mecca or Medina to pray? Why why why?" All the time, so would say this is 'farida' because we must do it, because it's right. It is written in the Quran. I remember, from when I was young, all the time I ask about our belief.

Based on similar encounters, MBB1 and MBB2 decided that they could no longer believe in God and, as a result, distanced themselves from their religion of birth as teenagers.

The interviewees indicated that their exposure to other cultures and religions, at an early age, is also a reason why they became critical towards Islam. MBB1 was sent to a regional district school and, as a result, "started thinking about the world." In a similar way, MBB2 moved to another city where she "started to see that it is a different life" when Jews, Muslims and Christians interact with one another in schools and neighbourhoods. During the interviews, it became evident that these members of the target group had had a longing – from an early age – for a society in which people of different cultures and religions can live together in peace and harmony. Since they have come to faith, it seems that this desire has only grown stronger. MBB3 indicated, for example, that "it is the calling. It is purpose to my life" to teach as a Muslim believer in Jesus at a Jewish school. Similarly, MBB1 attends an Arab Evangelical church and Messianic congregation to build bridges between both communities – a full description can be found in the interview summary report of her husband (AE3). Furthermore, they had given names to their children which are acceptable to their Muslim as well as Christian family members. This point was also made by MBB3 who indicated that she wants to give her children 'neutral' names in order to reduce the chance that they will experience racism in Israeli society because of their religious background. Overall, based on the answers provided during the interviews, it seems that these members of the target group considered their newly-found faith more compatible with their longing for a pluralistic society then their religion of birth.

7.3.2 Critical of Nominal Christianity, Longing for Evangelical Faith

The interviewees were introduced to the evangelical faith by a good friend (MBB2) or, at that time, their boyfriend (MBB1/MBB3). They had long conversations with these Arab Evangelicals and, eventually, they accepted their invitation to come to a church service (MBB1/MBB3) or Easter celebration (MBB2). On these occasions, they were challenged by the pastor to "come to Jesus" (MBB3) or to "ask Him" directly (MBB1/MBB2). One of the interviewees (MBB2) described this moment as follows:

> So, I kneeled and start talking to Him like I am talking to you. All of a sudden, I start crying. At that moment, I knew and felt that Jesus Christ is Lord. He is God. I cried I had never cried before.

The other interviewees had very similar experiences; MBB1 realised that, after hearing a sermon that addressed a specific and urgent need in her life, "of course there is God, he brought me at this point, he knows that I am feeling, what I am going through, this is not a coincidence, there is a God" and MBB3 recalled "I don't know how, I don't know why, I don't know anything, but I am just going [forward after the altar call]. From this time, I don't know what is happening. It was a lot of feelings." These spiritual encounters were instrumental in the conversion process of the interviewees. And, finally, each one of them indicated that reading the New Testament – although they found the crucifixion story very confusing – was crucial in their faith journey.

The reason that they became interested in attending a church service or holiday celebration was, first and foremost, caused by the difference they had observed between their evangelical friends and, more generally, nominal Christians. MBB1 saw, for example, the change of character in her boyfriend after he started attending a Arab Evangelical church, MBB2 was pleasantly surprised to find out that he could live in the dorms of the Anglican church and MBB3 already noticed at university, before she was a believer, "the difference between the really [nominal] Christians and the Christians that really follow Jesus". During the interviews, it became evident that these members of the target group made a clear distinction between nominal Christianity and Evangelicalism and, subsequently, were attracted towards the latter because of their contact with evangelical friends.

With regards to Diagram 2, MBB1 and MBB3 had difficulty with placing themselves in the Christian circle – possibly for the reasons mentioned above – although one of them (MBB3) had no problem calling herself a Christian. When asked specifically, they indicated that they prefer to describe themselves as follows: "I am from a Muslim family but I follow Jesus" (MBB1) or "I am a Muslim who believes in Jesus" (MBB3). In the end, these two Jesus followers placed themselves in J. The response of MBB2 was completely different, he positioned himself without hesitation in the Christian circle both in Diagram 1 and 2 – although he acknowledges that other believers might need more time to move from C to I to A – because "I put my Christianity before every identity" and "I sometimes forget that I was a Muslim". Even though he attends a Messianic congregation and observes the Jewish festivals, he does this "out of the knowledge of Jesus, not because of Judaism. We can see in each festival Jesus right there." MBB1 takes a similar approach to the Jewish feasts but, at the same time, also celebrates the Christian holidays. During the interview, MBB3 said that she has requested to be off from work during Christmas, because she wants to help out at the church fair and she finds "it is more beautiful". However, she also described the difficulty of no longer observing the Islamic holidays. She said: "this year [with Ramadan] I felt I am not a part of this group. And it was very hard. I live with my family." In terms of terminology, the interviewees do not use anymore the Islamic name of Jesus – i.e. *Isa* – but prefer to call him *Yesua* in Arabic. The Hebrew name of Jesus – i.e. *Yeshua* – was also commonly used by MBB1 and MBB2.

The change from their religion of birth to evangelical faith had not been without cost for the interviewees. MBB1 explained that, after her parents found out she and her husband are *mutajaddidiin* – i.e. the Arabic term for 'born-again' – the following happened:

> From that point, in 2008, there was a wall in our relationship, especially between me and my father. My mother was struggling a lot, but more accepting. The children made my parents closer to us. He would talk to my husband, but not to me just "hello". Nothing else. It is hard, it is better now, praise God.

Also, the family of MBB2 – although he considers them open-minded – he reported that they said "Don't bring us shame, whatever you want to believe, keep it away from the family." MBB3 has not shared with her family yet that she has come to faith in Jesus – only with her sister – but she found that her colleagues, nominal Christians, do not accept that she has become a Christian and continue to call her Muslim. From the interviews, it is clear that these Muslim-background believers experienced trials and adversity as a result of their conversion.

In closing, this chapter has provided an overview of the main themes that emerged from the interviews conducted with members of the target groups in this field study. The findings will be discussed, with regards to the central research question and sub-questions, in the following chapter.

8:   Discussion

Based on the data collected through the literature review and the data generated during the field study, the central research question and sub-questions will be answered in this chapter.[190] Furthermore, the implications for the field of missiology will be discussed and recommendations for further research will be made.

8.1   Sub-Questions

In this section, the sub-questions will be restated and, subsequently, answered for each target group individually. Only with the third sub-question, a comparison will be made between the personal and collective experiences of the members of these communities of evangelical faith with regards to their identity formation.

8.1.1   *Continuity* versus *Discontinuity*

The first sub-question is stated as follows: "In what way do members of the target groups encounter levels of *continuity* and/or *discontinuity* in their core, social and corporate identities with regards to their cultural and religious backgrounds?"

Messianic Jews in Israel continue, predominantly, to identify themselves as Jewish; both ethnically and culturally (§4.1). A number of the interviewees even indicated that they feel more Jewish since they have come to faith in their Messiah (§7.1.1). However, there seems to be a general tendency among Israeli Messianic Jews to distance themselves from Rabbinic Judaism (§4.1.2). For example, they prefer to observe the biblical holidays and commandments rather than the religious customs and traditions of the rabbis. Nevertheless, they continue to feel part of the people of Israel and play an active role in Israeli society. Their political views seem to even intensify as a result of their newly-found faith – especially with regards to 'the land' – even though they experience pressure, both personally and collectively, as members of a religious minority group in the State of Israel (§4.1.3). Interestingly, their sense of belonging is no longer limited to the Jewish people

---

[190] It should be noted that the findings of the field study cannot be generalised, due to the small scope of the research project, but they will be used to fill the gaps within in the literature and to verify or perhaps modify some of the results from the literature review.

because they also feel a strong connection with believers of evangelical faith from other cultural and religious backgrounds (§4.1.2). This is most clearly demonstrated with regards to their views on intermarriage; faith in Jesus is considered more important than ethnicity. Although Israeli Messianic Jews do not call themselves 'evangelicals', the majority of them do feel a strong connection with the evangelical world (§4.1.2). However, this seems to be more related to doctrinal beliefs than faith practice. By and large, they prefer to use Hebraic terminology – for example: 'Yeshua' rather than 'Jesus' – and hold on to a number of Judaic rituals, such as *bar/bat mitzvah* (§4.1.2). Furthermore, they attend Messianic congregations rather than Evangelical churches (§2.1). Although Messianic Jews in Israel experience *discontinuity* in terms of their core, social and corporate identities – i.e. believing in *Yeshua*, belonging to a community of evangelical faith, and being a member of a minority group in society – they encounter levels of *continuity* with regards to their ethnic, cultural and religious background.

Arab Evangelicals in Israel experience *discontinuity* in their social identity in relation to their community of birth. Although they do occasionally celebrate Christmas and Easter with their family members in the traditional churches, which was confirmed by the participants in the interviews (§7.2.2), they have drawn a clear boundary between their own faith and their religion of birth (§4.2.3). The label 'evangelical' serves, as such, as an identity marker (§3.5). Subsequently, they encounter even more difficulties in their daily lives as members of a 'minority of a minority of a minority' group (§2.2). This can be considered a point of *discontinuity* in their collective identity. Based on the field study, there also seems to be a great concern among Arab Evangelicals for the salvation of their non-believing family members, friends, colleagues, youth in their churches, and so forth (§7.2.1). Subsequently, they expressed a strong desire to be or are already involved in evangelism. This outcome from the field study confirms the strong ties between these believers of evangelical faith and the Protestant mission (§3.3). Other levels of *discontinuity* the interviewees encounter in their core and social identity are related to the importance they ascribe to personal faith and church attendance (§7.2). With regards to their collective identity, Arab Evangelicals seem to follow the socio-religious trend among Arab Christians by focussing more on their religion than on their ethnicity and nationality (§4.2.1). It is unclear, if they encounter any level of *discontinuity* with regards to their integration into Israeli society – as a means for Westernisation – but it is not unreasonable to assume that their involvement in evangelical Protestantism has given them more access to the West and, therefore, they do not perceive Israel as a means to this end (§4.2.2). If this notion is accurate, they will have encountered levels of *discontinuity* with regards to their core and collective identities. From the field study, it is clear that the gospel call – as presented by evangelicals from 'outside' – has had a profound effect on the personal lives of the interviewees and, eventually, resulting in a decision to leave their religion of birth and join a community of evangelical faith (§7.2).

Muslim-background believers in Israel encounter high levels of *discontinuity* in their social identity from the moment they make their newly-found faith public. More often than not, they become 'marginal believers' because they are no longer considered full members of their community and religion of birth and, at the same time, they are not fully welcomed as new members in the traditional and evangelical churches (§3.4). Although the interviews demonstrated that this might not always be the case, it seems to be rather an exception than common practice (§7.2.1). With regards to their core identity, Muslim-background believers in Israel become (more) religious as a result of their conversion (§4.3.2). Naturally, this has a great impact on their daily lives as they start to pray, read the Bible, join meetings with other believers of evangelical faith, and so forth. As such, they encounter levels of *discontinuity* in their core and social identity. From the interviews, it seems that these members of the target group find their newly-found faith more compatible with their longing for a pluralistic society than their religion of birth (§7.3.1). In this sense, there is a level of *continuity* with regards to this deeply held desire but they experience a level of *discontinuity* in relation to finding the means to this end. Furthermore, in accordance with the findings of the literature review (§4.3.2), the field study seems to verify that Muslim-background believers in the Holy Land become less political after they have come to faith. With regards to the festivals, the participants of the field study indicated that they no longer observe the holidays of their religion of birth but celebrate the feasts of their new community of evangelical faith (§7.3.2). Finally, the interviewees no longer use Islamic terminology – such as: *Isa* to refer to Jesus – or give their children Muslim names (§7.3.1). Even though it is unclear whether these levels of (*dis*)*continuity* are experienced by all Muslim-background believers in Israel, the field study has offered some interesting indications with regards to the first sub-question.

Overall, the data generated through the field study verifies, to a great extent, the findings of the literature review regarding the first sub-question. However, the effect of spiritual encounters (MJs), the ongoing influence of the Protestant mission (AE) and the impact of a strong desire for a pluralistic society (MBBs) on the levels of discontinuity – experienced by the members of the target groups – have emerged from this field study and need to be further explored.

8.1.2 *New* versus *Renewed*

The second sub-question is stated as follows: "In what way do members of the target groups pursue a *new* and/or *renewed* identity as Jesus followers?"

Messianic Jews in Israel *describe* their faith journey as 'returning to Zion', according to Warshawsky, but they seem to *experience* a religious conversion as they encounter 'newness' rather than 'renewal' (§4.1.3). Therefore, they pursue – perhaps unknowingly – a *new* rather than a *renewed* identity. However, this is in sharp contrast with their own narrative of their faith journey. During the interviews of the field study, this tension became also noticeable (§7.1.2). The participants indicated that they feel more Jewish than before, but at the same time they want to distance themselves from Rabbinic Judaism. The historical overview of Jesus-believing Jews provides some insights into why this might be the case (§2.1). The parting(s) of the ways has caused a clear division between these religions but, at the same time, might also have created a common terminology between the members of these religious communities as they were differentiating themselves from each other. In this way, the separation between Rabbinic Judaism and Christianity might have prevented the possibility of Jews pursuing a *renewed* identity as Jesus followers within their community and religion of birth, and would have left the pursuit of a *new* identity as the only option available. Subsequently, Jesus-believing Jews have been forced to cross boundaries between both religions and, therefore, they might feel that they have to find a 'third way' in order to mark the boundaries of their newly-found faith. Therefore, they can only pursue a *new* identity and are prevented from seeking a *renewed* identity. Although recent research seems to suggest that these factors might still be at play among Israeli Messianic Jews today (§4.1), the data of the field study demonstrates that the interviewees seek a *renewed* rather than a *new* identity (§7.1.2). As such, it verifies the findings of Warshawsky but it does not provide evidence that they are encountering *newness* rather than *renewal* (§4.1.3)

Arab Evangelicals in Israel seem to draw clear boundaries between their religion of birth and their community of evangelical faith (§2.2). From the literature review, and later on verified by the field study, there is no indication that they pursue a *renewed* identity but rather seek a *new* identity. One of the reasons for this phenomenon might be related to the fact that the majority of them left the traditional church of their upbringing in order to join – perhaps encouraged by foreign mission workers – an Evangelical church (§4.2.3). Subsequently, they have encountered increased hardship because they started to belong to a minority group (evangelicals) within a minority group (Christians) within a minority group (Arabs) in the State of Israel (§2.2) – which was confirmed by the participants of the field study (§7.2.1). Their decision for *institutional transition* has been costly and, therefore, they might be more inclined to pursue a *new* identity as Arab Evangelicals (§1.5). Furthermore, the Evangelical churches are closely connected to and, consequently, heavily influenced by Protestant denominations from Europe and North America (§3.5). Therefore, members might have adopted – perhaps rather willingly – an increasingly western mindset with its seemingly dualistic tendencies. In the interviews, there were traces visible of this possible change in worldview as the participants referred frequently to the differences between *before* and *after* their conversion; especially with regards to sin and personal faith (§7.2.1). Although no generalisation can be made from the findings of this field study, as pointed out before, this seems to be an interesting point of inquiry.

Muslim-background believers in Israel might find themselves unable to pursue a *new* and/or *renewed* identity because of the pressure they encounter from their friends and family members. More often than not, Jesus followers in the House of Islam do not have the freedom to decide whether they want to leave the mosque in order to join an Evangelical church or, conversely, practice their evangelical faith within their community and religion of birth (§4.3). Therefore, these Jesus followers are forced to form a hybrid identity that is acceptable to their family and friends if they are not able or prepared to leave everything behind to pursue a *new* identity (§4.3.1). Although there is not sufficient data on the situation of Muslim-background believers in Israel with regards to this issue, it is reasonable to assume and seemingly verified by the findings of the field study that they encounter similar issues as Jesus followers elsewhere in the Ummah. Furthermore, as pointed out before, the poor welcome they receive in the traditional and evangelical churches might lead them to sincerely question if they can even pursue a *new* identity even if they wanted to (§2.3). Another reason why members of the target group might not seek a *new* identity is related to the fact that most of them do not belong to an Evangelical church and, subsequently, are not exposed to Protestant theology with its seemingly dualistic tendencies. Therefore, they might even be unaware of the (possible) reasons or (perceived) necessity to leave their religion of birth in order to pursue a *new* identity as a believer of evangelical faith. On the other hand, however, the question could also be asked whether these Jesus followers even want to pursue a *renewed* identity within the House of Islam if they, mostly, were non-observant Muslims before they came to faith in Jesus. From the field study, it is clear that the interviewees are not interested in practicing their newly-found faith within their religion and community of birth (§7.3.1). They were mostly attracted to Jesus because of the believers of evangelical faith they met before and during their conversion processes (§7.3.2). Therefore, pursuing a *new* identity might be more appealing to these Jesus followers in Israel. This finding from the field study might be significant and could clarify, or even modify, the current understanding on this issue within the field of missiology.

Although the findings in this section carry some weight and are not without merit, the author is aware that the distinction between *new* and *renewed* can be considered ambiguous. Arguably, these terms are not binary opposites as is the case with the categories of the other two sub-questions – i.e. *continuity* versus *discontinuity* and *similarities* versus *dissimilarities*. The pilot project already demonstrated the challenges around the second sub-question but, as pointed out by the author before, the literature provided enough evidence to explore this issue further (§6.3). Within the scope of this thesis, the author has made an attempt to provide new and relevant insights on this topic. Further research will have to confirm whether a distinction can actually be made between a *new* and *renewed* identity – and to what extent this is relevant for the personal and collective experiences of members of the target groups – but, according to the author, the findings of this thesis support rather than discard this possibility.

8.1.3 *Similarities* versus *Dissimilarities*

The third sub-question is stated as follows: "In what way do members of the target groups form their identity in a *similar* and/or *dissimilar* way?"

From the answers provided above and from the findings of the literature review and field study, there are a number of *dissimilarities* in the way members of the target groups form their identities.

Firstly, MJs and AEs continue to observe a number of the holidays of their religion of birth. However, this does not seem to be the case with MBBs and, as a result, their social and collective identity might be formed differently (§8.1.1).

Secondly, MJs become more politically engaged after they have come to faith while the opposite seems to be the case with AEs and MBBs (§8.1.1). The reason for this might be related to their reading of the Scriptures but also, possibly, to their somewhat different status as a minority group within the state of Israel. The community of Messianic Jews is the largest in number and the closest to the majority group – i.e. Israeli Jews – of the three target groups and, therefore, they could have developed a stronger collective identity as a community of evangelical faith in the State of Israel (§3.4). Subsequently, they might feel that they have more influence in society and a role to play within the political system while the opposite might be the case for members of the other two target groups.

Thirdly, AEs emphasise their religion over their ethnicity – in accordance with a general socio-religious trend among Arab Christians – while MJs indicate that they feel more Jewish because their ethnicity is no longer defined by Rabbinic Judaism (§8.1.1). The position of MBBs with regards to this issue is unknown and would be an interesting topic for further research. Either way, both perspectives must have a profound impact on the formation of the core identity of members of each target group – as became evident during the interviews (§7.1.3/§7.2.1).

Fourthly, MJs and AEs stress the importance of attending a Messianic congregation or Evangelical church while MBBs remain largely unaffiliated (§8.1.1). Therefore, the core and social identity of MBBs seems to be less influenced by evangelical Protestantism while the opposite is clearly noticeable among MJs and AEs. With regards to this point, the field study seems to verify the findings of the literature review.

Fifthly, and arguably related to the previous point, MJs perceive their identity formation in terms of 'renewal' while AEs clearly pursue a 'new' identity MBBs seem to be unconcerned with this issue or are unable to choose between these two options of identity formation because of the hostile environment in which they practice their newly-found faith. As argued before, the field study seems to both verify and modify some of the findings from the literature review (§8.1.2).

The *dissimilarities* in identity formation among members of the target groups were also noticeable during the interviews, especially when they were asked to position themselves in Diagram 1 (Q17). It was during this exercise that the differences between members of these three communities of evangelical faith became more apparent – as visualised in Figure 4. The MJs consider themselves part of the Jewish circle (B), AEs struggle to place themselves inside or outside of the Christian circle (A) and MBBs only want to belong to this circle if it does not include nominal Christians. However, these Jesus followers from the House of Islam definitely do not see themselves as part of the Muslim circle (C). In summary, members of the target groups form their identities in various ways and some of the *dissimilarities* are clearly visible in the way they observe their holidays, shape their political views, value their ethnicity, and pursue their new/renewed identity.

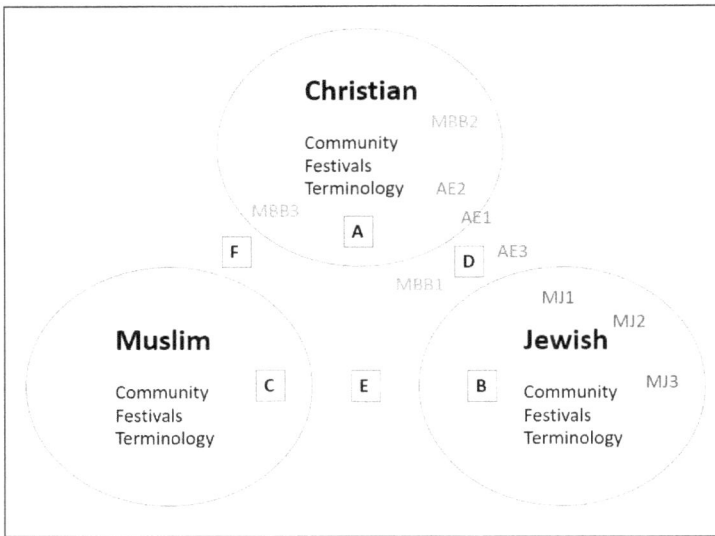

Figure 4: Diagram I

There are also a number of *similarities* observable among members of the target groups with regards to their identity formation. Firstly, they continue to feel connected to their community of birth (§8.1.1). This is perhaps surprising because they are no longer considered full members by the other adherents due to the fact they have moved away – to some extent – from their religion of birth. Naturally, this change in their affiliation has an impact on the way they form their core and social identities. Secondly, they no longer use some of the terminology of their community or religion of birth. For example, in the interviews Jesus was called 'son of God' (MBBs), 'Lord' (AEs) or 'Messiah' (MJs) rather than 'prophet' (Muslims), 'son of Mary' (Christians) or 'may his name and memory be blotted out' (Jews). Furthermore, the interviewees do not call themselves anymore by their ethnicity or religion of birth only – i.e. Jew, Arab Christian, Muslim – but add a word to indicate that they are Jesus followers, such as: 'Messianic Jew', 'Arab Evangelical', 'believer from a Muslim family', and so forth. In this way, the literature was verified by the findings of the field study. Thirdly, their personal faith and doctrinal beliefs have become the determining factor regarding to whom they belong. In the interviews, this became evident when the question about intermarriage was asked (Q23). Ultimately, evangelical faith is considered more important than ethnicity in choosing a husband or wife. This also became clear in the answers provided to question 24. When asked to position themselves in Diagram 2, they indicated – by and large – that circle J and G is the closest to their daily experiences as believers of evangelical faith in the north of Israel. Regardless of their ethnic, social, cultural and religious backgrounds the majority of them find themselves in the circles that bind them together with other Jesus followers – as visualised in Figure 5. By their own account, this is caused by their common faith in Jesus and the communities of evangelical faith to which they belong. From this perspective, it could be argued that the interviewees have formed their core, social and corporate identities in a *similar* way, because each one of them indicated that they experience – in their daily lives – a closer connection and stronger sense of belonging to other believers of evangelical faith than to members of their own community and religion of birth.

In conclusion, the (dis)similarities in the identity formation of members of the target groups have become evident in answering the third sub-question. By adapting the diagrams of Green (§6.1), visualising the data generated from the interviews (Figure 4 & 5), comparing the personal and collective experiences of members of three target groups, and verifying or modifying the findings of the literature review based on the outcomes of the field study (§8.1), this thesis has provided a unique contribution to the field of missiology.

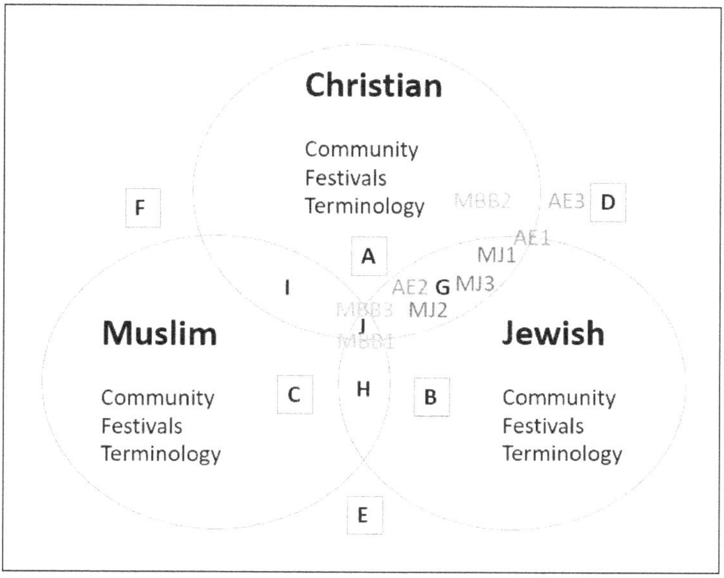

Figure 5: Diagram 2

8.2   Central Research Question

The central research question is stated as follows: "How can the identity formation of Messianic Jews, Arab Evangelicals and Muslim-background believers in Israel be described and in what way are their personal and collective experiences similar and/or dissimilar in this domain?"

As discussed in the literature review, two major studies have used the metaphor of 'traveling' and 'spiritual migration' as a way to describe the identity formation of Jesus followers from Jewish and Muslim backgrounds (§4.1.3/§4.3.1). Comparing the personal and collective experiences of the members of these target groups necessitates a discussion of whether the formation of their core, social and corporate identities can be described in terms of 'being on a journey' and, by extension, whether they are walking along the same routes, towards a common destination, crossing or marking similar borders in the process, required to leave behind comparable possessions before and during embarking on this journey, and are welcomed in the same way once they arrive.

Based on the findings of this thesis, it seems that some parts of their faith journey appear to be similar, but not all. They might have the same destination in mind but, at times, take different routes. MJs indicate that they want to return to Zion – and, therefore, pursue a *renewed* identity – while AEs are longing for the heavenly Jerusalem and, hence, are more interested in seeking a *new* identity. MBBs, however, appear to be largely unaware of the possible routes they can take to the mountain of the Lord because they are faced with too much rubble on the way. Getting there unharmed seems to be more important than the destination itself. Also, the borders that must be crossed by each group of Jesus followers are not entirely the same either. Although they are all accused of entering a foreign land by members of their respective communities of birth, MJs rather experience a return to their homeland. AEs, however, do feel the need to enter a new land and MBBs seem to wonder if they will ever come home at all. Interestingly, however, when they encounter each other along the road, they tend to feel a strong sense of connection and belonging to one another. They are even willing to set out new territories and mark boundaries through marriage and other faith-based activities. They are even accustomed to using the same language when they talk about Jesus – although it might sound differently in their mother tongue – and even celebrate religious holidays together, occasionally, as long as they are centred around the Messiah. Although there remains a level of suspicion, especially with regards to each other's political views and affiliations, there is a bond of brother and sisterhood when they meet each other as fellow travellers on a faith journey.

As demonstrated above, the identity formation of Messianic Jews, Arab Evangelicals and Muslim-background believers can be described in terms of 'being on a journey' but this does not mean that their personal and collective experiences are entirely the same along this faith journey. There are *similarities* as well as *dissimilarities* in the way that they form their core, social and corporate identities. However, there is a sense of connection and belonging when they encounter each other as believers of evangelical faith.

8.3   Implications for the Field of Missiology

Based on the findings and the discussion of this thesis, the implications of this comparative study for the field of missiology should also be explored.

First, scholars and practitioners need to exercise care when assuming that the personal and collective experiences of Messianic Jews and Muslim-background believers – with regards to identity formation – are similar. This thesis has demonstrated that this is the case in regards to some aspects of their core, social and corporate identities but not entirely. As pointed out in §3.6, missiologists regularly draw comparisons between these two groups of Jesus followers without providing sufficient evidence to support their claims. The same can be said for parallels drawn between the experiences of the first disciples – i.e. Jesus-believing Jews in Second Temple Judaism – and Jesus followers in Insider Movements. This thesis has demonstrated that these comparisons do not hold without sufficient evidence.

Secondly, this thesis has shown that a comparative study between members of these target groups provides a rare opportunity to gain more understanding on a number of missiological issues. These communities of evangelical faith in Israel form a unique sample group for a comparative study in the field of missiology. For example, missiologists could conduct a research project on the effects of Protestant theology on Messianic Jews and Arab Evangelicals and, at the same time, the absence of this theology from the 'outside' among Muslim-background believers. In a similar way, the reasons behind Insider Movements can be researched among Muslim-background believers in Israel and, simultaneously, why this method of contextualisation does not seem to appeal to Israeli Messianic Jews. This selection of examples serves to illustrate that the presence of these communities of evangelical faith within a small geographical area provides a unique opportunity for comparative studies in the field of missiology.

Thirdly, and lastly, a number of relevant topics and interesting insights have emerged throughout the course of this research project. Although these will be discussed in more detail below (§8.4), there is a strong sense that more research is required to gain a better understanding of a number of key issues within the field of missiology. In this first attempt to compare the personal and collective experiences of members of these communities of evangelical faith in Israel, it has become evident that scholars and practitioners can receive much insight from listening to the narratives and experiences of these Jesus followers in the Holy Land. Therefore, the author of this thesis would contend that there is an urgent need for this research to be built upon by other scholars in the field of missiology.

8.4   Recommendations for Further Research

This thesis has provided an in-depth review of the literature available on the identity formation of Messianic Jews, Arab Evangelicals and Muslim-background believers in Israel. Furthermore, a field study was conducted as a first attempt to compare the personal and collective experiences of members of these target groups in this domain and, thereby, filling a gap within the literature. Whilst more research is required to verify the findings of this thesis and to gain a better understanding of the formation of their core, social and corporate identities, this study has provided a number of significant and noteworthy insights which can be further explored. In this final section a number of suggestions will be made for further research.

First, the metaphor of 'being on a journey' has been used in this research project to describe the identity formation of these Jesus followers in Israel. It would be interesting to find out if this terminology is also prominent in their theology or liturgy and, subsequently, if this is related to the biblical notion of 'being a sojourner on this earth'.[191] Furthermore, research could be conducted on the ancient practice and belief of 'pilgrimage' throughout Church history in connection to the identity negotiation among members of the target groups. In a similar way, exegetical studies on this particular topic and – more generally – on *identity formation* might provide new insights for these Jesus followers.[192]

---

[191]   For example: Philippians 3:20; Hebrews 11:13-16; 2 Corinthians 5:1-10; Hebrews 13:14

[192]   The author recommends Tucker & Baker's handbook as a starting point for a general inquiry into the issue of identity formation from the field of Biblical Studies. Furthermore, Campbell's study on Christian identity from the teachings of apostle Paul, addresses many of the topics – especially chapter 9 – discussed in this thesis, most notably: (dis)continuity, collective versus individual, conversion from an ancient and modern perspective, and so forth. J. Brian Tucker and Coleman A. Baker,

Secondly, there is a noticeable tension between the academic discourse in the West and the daily experiences of Jesus followers in Israel. This can be observed in the way that identity theories seem to focus primarily on the perspective of the individual rather than the collective. Similarly, religious acts that demonstrate a personal faith seem to be considered signs of a genuine conversion but the question could be asked if these carry the same weight in a community-based society. In addition, more generally, there also seems to be a noticeable tension between the dualistic tendencies of a Western mindset versus a holistic approach to life and faith in the Middle East – as discussed in §6.3 and §8.1.2. It would be interesting to investigate how these differences in perspectives and worldviews have an effect on missiological research in general and, more specifically, on the identity formation of Jesus followers in Israel.[193]

Thirdly, many members of the target groups encounter a change in their social status as a result of their decision to follow Jesus. As highlighted in this thesis, this is an experience they share and, arguably, it brings them together as members of minority groups. This issue needs to be further researched, especially with regards to their *sense of belonging* and *coping strategies*. Are their experiences, for example, different from others who have gone through a similar socio-religious change in Israel society? Do members of the target groups have a similar connection with them or is this only the case with those who belong to a community of evangelical faith?

Fourthly, it would be interesting to find out what the differences are in identity formation between first- and second-generation believers between the target groups. As two of the three communities of evangelical faith – i.e. Messianic Jews and Muslim-background believers – are in the early stages of their development, it would be beneficial to find out which lessons can be learned from the establishment of the Arab Evangelical community in Israel over the last hundred and fifty years.

Fifthly, the similarities and dissimilarities between the identity formation of members of the target groups have been demonstrated and visualised in §8.1.3. An interesting topic for further research would be to explore the sense of awareness of these (dis)similarities among believers of evangelical faith in Israel. Do they see themselves as fellow travellers on a

---

eds., *T&T Clark Handbook to Social Identity in the New Testament* (London: Bloomsbury, 2014).; William S. Campbell, *Paul and the Creation of Christian Identity*, T & T Clark Biblical Studies (London ; New York: T & T Clark, 2008).

[193] William A. Dyrness, *Insider Jesus: Theological Reflections on New Christian Movements* (Downers Grove, Illinois: IVP Academic, an imprint of InterVarsity Press, 2016).

faith journey? Are there any indications that they might take, at times, different routes on purpose?

Sixthly, for reasons already mentioned in §8.3, missiological topics related to contextualisation – such as: 'Insider Movements' – should be researched among the members of these target groups. The presence of three communities of evangelical faith in Israel provides a unique opportunity to conduct a comparative study on these topics of missiological interest.

Any comparative study on topics presented in this section will require a substantial amount of new data. Therefore, it would be most fitting to dedicate a doctoral dissertation (PhD) to this kind of research project.

In this chapter, the central research question and sub-questions have been answered, the implications for the field of missiology have been addressed and recommendations have been made for further research.

9:   Conclusion

This research project has been a first attempt to compare the identity formation of Messianic Jews, Arab Evangelicals and Muslim-background believers in Israel. In the final chapter of this thesis, an overview will be provided of how the answers to the central research questions and subquestions were reached and reflections will be offered on the outcomes of this comparative study.

9.1   Research Process

The author of this thesis became aware of a research gap in the field of missiology through his personal experience of ministering in Israel and his review of the available literature. Although the identity formation of Jesus followers from a Jewish, Christian and Muslim background has been researched quite extensively, no comparative study was available on the personal and collective experiences of Messianic Jews, Arab Evangelicals and Muslim-background believers in this domain. Due to the points of commonality between these Jesus followers in Israel, the author of this thesis became interested in comparing the formation of their core, social and corporate identities. The literature review revealed the need for a comparative study between members of these target groups because of the history, culture(s), language(s), worldview(s) and political struggles they share. Furthermore, many of these Jesus followers have been greatly influenced by Protestant theology and mission. Their history and points of commonality were analysed in chapters 2 and 3, and an overview of the studies on identity formation was provided in chapter 4.

Based on the literature review, a missiological framework for a comparative study was presented in chapter 5. Relevant *concepts* – such as, 'identity-as-travel', 'spiritual migration' and 'three layers of identity' – were selected and *themes* – i.e. (dis)continuity, (re)new(ed), (dis)similarities – and were specified in order to compare the identity formation of the members of these target groups. This missiological framework for a comparative study was, subsequently, tested through a pilot project in Belgium and used for a field study in the north of Israel. The methodology behind these research projects was discussed in chapter 6.

Although the field study was limited in scope, the findings provided a number of interesting and meaningful insights on the identity formation of members of these target groups and these were, subsequently, presented in chapter 7. This data was generated in order to confirm or challenge the outcomes of the literature review and, furthermore, to fill the gaps within this area of missiological research. The discussion in chapter 8 demonstrated that this was more necessary than anticipated beforehand, because there seems to be – to some extent – a discrepancy between academic research and the daily experiences of Jesus followers in Israel. By highlighting some of these differences in the discussion, a more balanced answer could be provided to the central research question and subquestions.

In conclusion, the identity formation of Messianic Jews, Arab Evangelicals and Muslim-background believers can be described in terms of 'being on a journey'. Although they might have the same destination in mind, they do not always take identical routes or cross the same borders. However, there are similar elements in their faith journey and, as result, there is a strong sense of connection and belonging when they encounter each other as fellow travellers.

9.2   Outcomes of this Thesis

The objectives of this thesis were, first of all, to collect the data available on the identity formation of members of the target groups through a literature review and, secondly, to generate new data on the formation of their core, social and corporate identities through a field study. Although the scope of this research project had its limitations, it has offered an initial attempt to compare the personal and collective experiences of these Jesus followers in this domain. By doing so, it has given a unique insight into some of the similarities and dissimilarities faced by believers of evangelical faith in Israel. In this way, the objectives of this thesis have been achieved.

This research project has made a unique and valuable contribution to the field of missiology, because it has generated new and rich data on the identity formation of believers of evangelical faith in Israel and, subsequently, verified or modified some of the findings of the literature review. Furthermore, it has provided a missiological framework for a comparative study between members of these target groups and has been, subsequently, tested in a pilot project and used in a field study. In this way, the framework can serve as a model for further research among these communities of evangelical faith in Israel and beyond.

Finally, this thesis has drawn awareness to some of the issues at play within the field of missiology with regards to conducting research crossculturally. Some of the same difficulties are observable in the history of Protestant mission in the Holy Land since the eighteenth century. Greater awareness about these cross-cultural issues by scholars and practitioners will be beneficial for all who are concerned about the growth and well-being of communities of evangelical faith in the Middle East.

9.3   Personal Reflections

Over the last three years, the author of this thesis has dedicated a significant amount of his time and energy to gain a better understanding of the identity formation of Messianic Jews, Arab Evangelicals and Muslim-background believers in Israel. In conclusion, he will share a number of personal reflections on the process and outcomes of his thesis.

Firstly, the author became increasingly aware of the tension between being an 'outsider' as well as an someone who is and has been occasionally on the 'inside', as the research project progressed. Although he had explored this issue beforehand, as discussed in §1.6 and §6.2, its significance became only evident in the later stages of writing his thesis. The *benefits* of being acquainted with the target groups were clearly demonstrated by his access to these communities of evangelical in Israel and his ability to converse with the members in their own language. However, the *drawbacks* of being closely connected to the target groups – most notably, the inability of the researcher to distance himself from the personal and collective experiences of the members and to take a neutral stance towards some of the more sensitive issues – became also noticeable. For example, he seriously struggled with using some of the academic terminology – such as 'conversion' and 'evangelical' – because of the great sensitivity around these words among Jesus followers in Israel. However, throughout his thesis, the author has tried to use these terms as objectively and consistently as possible with the understanding that he would not be able to satisfy everyone with the choices he had to make. Overall, he realises that this research project could not have been conducted if he had been merely an 'outsider' but, at the same time, he underestimated the difficulty of being, although occasionally, on the 'inside' as a researcher.

Secondly, the author found it a constant struggle to define the limits of his research project. He wanted to be as comprehensive as possible with regards to the literature available and, at the same time, he needed to be disciplined in using only the data relevant to the central research question and sub-questions. This proved to be a major challenge on numerous occasions throughout the research project. When he explained the topic of his thesis to other students or professors, they would always respond in a similar way: "It sounds like you need to do a PhD". Although this was not intended, the author realised early on in the research process that the topic of his thesis might require this kind of scope and attention. Especially with regards to his field study, he would have preferred to conduct a larger number of semi-structured interviews in order to generate more data. However, this was not possible within the given time frame of his research project. He sincerely hopes that someone else will take up the mantle and continue to research the identity formation of believers of evangelical faith in Israel and, more generally, the Middle East. From his personal experience, the author believes it is important that more research will be done in this area in order to gain a better understanding of how these Jesus followers can be discipled.

Thirdly, the author of this thesis was given the advice, on a number of occasions, to be more *descriptive* in his research project. Although he had a strong desire to find out what the most fruitful practice of identity formation is among Jesus followers in Israel – which is, he discovered, not uncommon for scholars in the field of missiology – he started to realise that this would require a different kind of research project.[194] Therefore, he has tried to avoid – as much as possible – being *normative* and, instead, made an attempt to *explore* rather than *discuss*. However, he still has a strong desire to find out which forms of identity formation are more fruitful than others and to gain a better understanding of what the Bible teaches about this topic. His longing for more clarity proved also to be a strong temptation throughout this research project because it was, more often than not, rather complicated to fully comprehend the personal and collective experiences of the members of these target groups. Even in describing the various aspects of their identity formation, the author had to make the decision to keep it 'messy' at times because the narratives of these Jesus followers were sometimes filled with contradictions and open endings. Most members of these target groups greatly struggled with forming their core, social and corporate identities and, as a result, their reasoning and decision-making is sometimes difficult to follow. In all of this, the author has tried to describe these processes as accurately as possible.

Finally, the author of this thesis has been greatly impacted by what he has read and heard throughout this research project. Like Greenlee – who

---

[194]   Little's dissertation on discipleship among Muslim-background believers might be a good example of this 'different kind of research project' as he combines Biblical studies with missiological research rather successfully. Donald Bruce Little, 'Effective Insider Discpling: Helping Arab World Believers From Muslim Backgrounds Persevere and Thrive in Community' (Hamilton, Gordon-Conwell Theological Seminary, 2009).

noticed at a Christian conference in Basel that German teenagers were asking the same kind of questions as Muslim-background believers around the
world – he found himself often in conversation with his friends in Belgium
and the Netherlands about the issues raised by these Jesus followers in Israel.[195] And, more often than not, he was challenged to reconsider his own
position and views on identity formation. It is an understatement to say
that the author has learned some of life's most valuable lessons from these
Jesus followers in Israel and beyond. He sometimes even wondered if they
might find themselves, sooner rather than later, leading the way for other
believers of evangelical faith around the world. These Jesus followers have
learned through trial and error how to form their identity in accordance
with the gospel and, as such, they seem to be forerunners in this endeavour.

It is the hope of this author that his thesis offers a unique and meaningful contribution to the research community, shares the lessons that he
has learned from members of the target groups with a wider audience,
serves as an encouragement to believers of evangelical faith in the Middle
East and around the world, and presents a fresh challenge to everyone who
considers him or herself a Jesus follower to re-examine the formation of
his or her identity in the Messiah.

---

[195] Greenlee, *Longing for Community*, XIII.

Bibliography

Ajaj, Azar, Duane Alexander Miller, and Philip Sumpter. *Arab Evangelicals in Israel*. Eugene, Oregon: Pickwick Publications, 2016.

Bailey, Betty Jane, and J. Martin Bailey. *Who Are the Christians in the Middle East?* Grand Rapids, Mich: W.B. Eerdmans, 2003.

Barnett, Jens. 'Conversion's Consequences: Identity, Belonging, and Hybridity amongst Muslim Followers of Christ [Unpublished Thesis]'. Redcliffe College, 2008.

———. 'Narrative, Identity and Discipleship'. *Musafir: A Bulletin of Intercultural Studies* 3, no. 2 (2009): 3–5.

———. 'Refusing to Choose: Multiple Belonging among Arab Followers of Christ'. In *Longing for Community: Church, Ummah, or Somewhere in Between?*, edited by David Greenlee, 19–28. Pasadena, CA: William Carey Library, 2013.

Bosch, David Jacobus. *Transforming Mission: Paradigm Shifts in Theology of Mission*. American Society of Missiology Series, no. 16. Maryknoll, N.Y: Orbis Books, 1991.

Bryman, Alan. *Social Research Methods*. Fifth edition. Oxford: Oxford University Press, 2016.

Calder, Mark Daniel. 'Palestinian Christians – Situating Selves in a Dislocated Present'. In *Routledge Handbook of Minorities in the Middle East*, edited by Paul S. Rowe, 100–114. Routledge Handbooks. London ; New York, NY: Routledge, 2019.

Campbell, William S. *Paul and the Creation of Christian Identity*. T & T Clark Biblical Studies. London ; New York: T & T Clark, 2008.

Cohn-Sherbok, Dan. *Messianic Judaism*. London ; New York: Continuum, 2000.

Cragg, Kenneth. *The Arab Christian: A History in the Middle East*. 1st ed. Louisville, Ky: Westminster/John Knox Press, 1991.

Dunning, Craig A. 'Palestinian Muslims Converting to Christianity: Effective Evangelistic Methods in the West Bank.' University of Pretoria, 2013.

Durie, Mark. 'Messianic Judaism and Deliverance'. In *Muslim Conversions to Christ: A Critique of Insider Movements in Islamic Contexts*, edited by Ayman S. Ibrahim and Ant B. Greenham, 265–83. New York: Peter Lang, 2018.

Dyrness, William A. *Insider Jesus: Theological Reflections on New Christian Movements*. Downers Grove, Illinois: IVP Academic, an imprint of InterVarsity Press, 2016.

Eidsheim, Christine. 'Negotiating a Messianic Identity: A Study on the Formation of Messianic Identity through Space, Art, and Language in Modern Israel [Unpublished Thesis]'. University of Oslo, 2019.

Feher, Shoshanah. *Passing over Easter: Constructing the Boundaries of Messianic Judaism*. Walnut Creek, CA: AltaMira Press, 1998.

Garrison, David. *A Wind in the House of Islam: How God Is Drawing Muslims around the World to Faith in Jesus Christ.* Monument, CO: WIGTake Resources, 2014.

Green, Tim. 'Conversion in the Light of Identity Theories'. In *Longing for Community: Church, Ummah, or Somewhere in Between?*, edited by David Greenlee, 41–52. Pasadena, CA: William Carey Library, 2013.

———. 'Identity Choices at the Border Zone'. In *Longing for Community: Church, Ummah, or Somewhere in Between?*, edited by David Greenlee, 53–66. Pasadena, CA: William Carey Library, 2013.

———. 'Identity Issues for Ex-Muslim Christians, with Particular Reference to Marriage'. *St Francis Magazine* 8, no. 4 (2012): 435–81.

———. 'Issues of Identity for Christians of a Muslim Background in Pakistan'. University of London, 2014.

Greenham, Ant. 'Muslim Conversions to Christ: An Investigation of Palestinian Converts Living in the Holy Land'. Southeastern Baptist Theological Seminary, 2004.

Greenlee, David. 'Living Out an "In Christ" Identity: Research and Reflections Related to Muslims Who Have Come to Faith in Jesus Christ'. *International Journal of Frontier Missiology* 30, no. 1 (2013): 5–12.

———, ed. *Longing for Community: Church, Ummah, or Somewhere in Between?* Pasadena, CA: William Carey Library, 2013.

Harvey, Richard. *Mapping Messianic Jewish Theology: A Constructive Approach.* Studies in Messianic Jewish Theology. Milton Keynes, U.K: Paternoster, 2009.

Ibrahim, Ayman S., and Ant B. Greenham, eds. *Muslim Conversions to Christ: A Critique of Insider Movements in Islamic Contexts.* New York: Peter Lang, 2018.

Jameson, Richard, and Nick Scalevich. 'First-Century Jews and Twentieth-Century Muslims'. *International Journal of Frontier Missiology* 17, no. 1 (2000): 33–39.

Kjaer-Hansen, Kai. 'An Introduction to the Names Yehoshua/Joshua, Yeshua, Jesus and Yeshu [Accessed 24/10/2019]', 1992. https://jewsforjesus.org/answers/an-introduction-to-the-names-yehoshua/joshua-yeshua-jesus-and-yeshu/.

———, ed. *Jewish Identity and Faith in Jesus.* Jerusalem: Caspari Center, 1996.

Kjaer-Hansen, Kai, and Bodil F. Skjøtt. *Facts & Myths about Messianic Congregations in Israel.* Miskan 30–31. Jerusalem: United Christian Council in Israel, 1999.

Kok, Jacobus (Kobus), and John Anthony Dunne, eds. *Insiders versus Outsiders: Exploring the Dynamic Relationship between Mission and Ethos in the New Testament.* Perspectives on Philosophy and Religious Thought 14. Piscataway: Gorgias Press, 2014.

Kraft, Kathryn Ann. 'Community and Identity among Arabs of a Muslim Background Who Choose to Follow a Christian Faith'. University of Bristol, 2007.

———. *Searching for Heaven in the Real World: A Sociological Discussion of Conversion in the Arab World.* Cork: Words By Design, 2013.

Larsen, Timothy, and Daniel J. Treier, eds. *The Cambridge Companion to Evangelical Theology*. Cambridge Companions to Religion. Cambridge New York: Cambridge University Press, 2007.

Lausanne Global Consulation. 'The Lausanne Rome 2018 Statement on Nominal Christianity [Accessed 10/11/2019]'. Rome, 2018. https://www.lausanne.org/content/statement/missing-christians-global-call.

Lawrence, Peter. 'Muslim-Background Believers in Belgium in Search of a Renewed Identity as Followers of Jesus, an Enquiry [Unpublished Field Study Project]'. ETF, Leuven, 2019.

Le Roi, J. F. A. De. *Evangelische Christenheit und die Juden*. Hansebooks, 2017.

Little, Donald Bruce. 'Effective Insider Discpling: Helping Arab World Believers From Muslim Backgrounds Persevere and Thrive in Community'. Gordon-Conwell Theological Seminary, 2009.

Massey, Joshua. 'Part I – Living like Jesus, a Torah-Observant Jew: Delighting in God's Law for Incarnational Witness to Muslims'. *International Journal of Frontier Missiology* 21, no. 1 (2004): 13–22.

———. 'Part II – Living like Jesus, a Torah-Observant Jew: Delighting in God's Law for Incarnational Witness to Muslims'. *International Journal of Frontier Missiology* 21, no. 2 (2004): 55–71.

Miller, Duane Alexander. 'Christians from a Muslim Background in the Middle East'. In *Routledge Handbook of Minorities in the Middle East*, edited by Paul S. Rowe, 132–45. Routledge Handbooks. London ; New York, NY: Routledge/Taylor & Francis Group, 2019.

———. *Living among the Breakage: Contextual Theology-Making and Ex-Muslim Christians*. Eugene, Oregon: Pickwick Publications, 2016.

Munayer, Salim. 'The Ethnic Identity of Palestinian Arab Christian Adolescents in Israel'. Oxford Centre for Mission Studies, 2000.

Munayer, Salim J., and Gabriel Horenczyk. 'Multi-Group Acculturation Orientations in a Changing Context: Palestinian Christian Arab Adolescents in Israel after the Lost Decade'. *International Journal of Psychology* 49, no. 5 (October 2014): 364–70.

Munayer, Salim, and Lisa Loden. *The Land Cries out: Theology of the Land in the Israeli-Palestinian Context*. Eugene, Or.: Cascade Books, 2012.

———. *Through My Enemy's Eyes: Envisioning Reconciliation in Israel-Palestine*, 2014.

Musalaha. 'Palestinian Christian Identity in Israel: New Trends of Research [Accessed 1/11/2019]'. Jerusalem, 2015. https://www.youtube.com/user/musalahagalil/videos.

Oksnevad, Roy. 'BMB Discipleship: An Investigation into the Factors Leading to Disharmony within the Iranian Churches in the Diaspora'. *St Francis Magazine* 8, no. 4 (2012): 397–434.

Pritz, Ray A. *Nazarene Jewish Christianity: From the End of the New Testament Period until Its Disappearance in the Fourth Century*. Jerusalem: Magnes Press, 1992.

Rambo, Lewis R., ed. *The Oxford Handbook of Religious Conversion*. Oxford ; New York: Oxford University Press, 2014.

———. *Understanding Religious Conversion*. New Haven: Yale University Press, 1993.

Reedijk, W. 'Roots and Routes: Identity Construction and the Jewish-Christian-Muslim Dialogue'. Vrije Universiteit Amsterdam, 2010.

Soref, Erez. 'The Messianic Jewish Movement in Modern Israel'. In *Israel, the Church, and the Middle East: A Biblical Response to the Current Conflict.*, edited by Darrell L Bock and Mitch Glaser, 137–50. Kregel Publications, 2018.

Stern, David H. *Messianic Jewish Manifesto*. Clarksville, MD: Jewish New Testament Publications, 1997.

Syrjänen, Seppo. *In Search of Meaning and Identity: Conversion to Christianity in Pakistani Muslim Culture*. Finnish Society for Missiology and Ecumenics 45. Helsinki: Finnish Society for Missiology and Ecumenics, 1984.

Talman, Harley, and John Travis, eds. *Understanding Insider Movements: Disciples of Jesus within Diverse Religious Communities*. Pasadena, CA: William Carey Library, 2015.

Thomas, David. 'Arab Christianity'. In *The Blackwell Companion to Eastern Christianity*, edited by Kenneth Parry, 1–22. Blackwell Companions to Religion. Malden, MA: Wiley-Blackwell, 2010.

Tucker, J. Brian, and Coleman A. Baker, eds. *T&T Clark Handbook to Social Identity in the New Testament*. London: Bloomsbury, 2014.

Van de Poll, Evert. *Sacred Times for Chosen People: Development, Analysis and Missiological Significance of Messianic Jewish Holiday Practice*. Mission, no. 46. Zoetermeer: Boekencentrum, 2008.

Verhoeven, Pieternella Susanna. *Doing research: the hows and whys of applied research*. Chicago: Lyceum Books, 2008.

Warshawsky, Keri Zelson. 'Returning To Their Own Borders; A Social Anthropological Study of Contemporary Messianic Jewish Identity in Israel'. The Hebrew University, 2008.

Appendix

Interview Guide

Introduction:

- I am conducting a number of interviews with believers in Israel for my master's thesis in Theology and Religious Studies at ETF in Leuven.[196]
- During this interview you do not have to answer any questions you feel uncomfortable with.
- Your name will be not be used in my research project, but pseudonyms will be assigned.
- Do I have your permission to record this interview?

Biographical opening: Can you tell me something about yourself? Where were you born and raised? What did you study? Are you married, single or in a relationship? Do you have children? In which languages are you able to converse? Who are your friends? What is your occupation?

Religious background:

1. What is your religion of birth?
2. What was your view of Christians/Evangelicals and Christianity/Evangelicalism before you became a believer in Jesus?
3. How seriously did you practice your faith? Were you a secular, cultural, nominal, traditional or religious Jew/Christian/Muslim?

Conversion (factors, processes and consequences):

4. How did you come to faith in Jesus?
5. How long did this process take? Do you remember the moment when you made a definite decision to follow Jesus?
6. How do you look back on your life before you became a believer? Positive or negative? Are there elements you miss from your former life?

---

[196] During the interview, the terms 'believer' and 'follower of Jesus' will be used to refer to Messianic Jews, Arab Evangelicals and Muslim-background believers.

7. Do you find your religion of birth a help or hindrance in your walk with Jesus?
8. If a Jew/Christian/Muslim wants to become a follower of Jesus, what should he do?
9. Who knows that you are a believer? How did they respond?
10. Do you sometimes feel that you have to avoid mentioning that you are a follower of Jesus?

Personal Identity:

11. What do you call yourself when describing your faith? Which term(s) do you use in your own language? For example: believer, follower of Jesus, Messianic Jew/Arab Evangelical/Muslim-background believer, Christian, Evangelical and so forth.
12. Ritual: Have you been baptised? If so, when? What difference, if any, did it make in your spiritual life?
13. Routine: How often do you pray and/or read your Bible? Do you find these (new) elements of your faith confusing or do you welcome them?
14. Rhetoric: How do you call God in your prayers? Which terms do you use in your language?
15. Badges of belonging: How do people know that you are a follower of Jesus? Do you have something visible (as a reminder that you belong to Jesus) that is also observable for others?

Social and Corporate Identity:

16. Who are:
    a) Israeli's/Palestinians? In what way are you an Israeli/Palestinian like that? (nationality)
    b) Jews/Arabs? In what way are you a Jew/Arab like that? (ethnicity)
    c) Believers? In what way are you a believer like that? (religious belief)
    d) MJs/AEs/MBBs? In what way are you a MJ/AE/MBB like that? (religious affiliation)
    e) Evangelicals? In what way are you an Evangelical like that? (religious family)

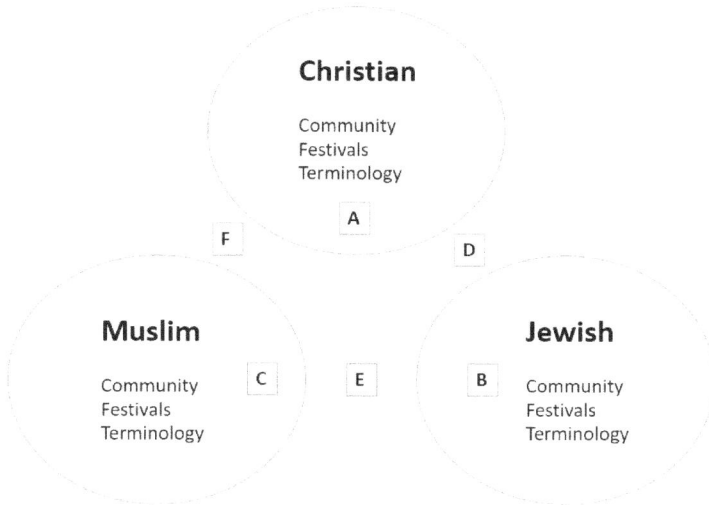

Diagram 1

17. Most people in Israel are born into either one of these three communities. Which position do you find yourself in most of the time (A, B or C) or are you switching between two circles (D, E or F)?
18. Do your relatives know that you spend time with believers? If so, do they mind?
19. Do you use different terminology when you interact with people from other communities?
20. Which religious and/or national festivals do you observe?
21. How often do you meet with believers; personally and/or corporately? Are they from a Jewish, Christian and/or Muslim background? Are you member of a congregation/church/ fellowship?
22. How does your faith influence your political views?
23. Do you want to marry/are you married to a (believing) Jew/Arab/ Muslim? Do you give/have you given your children Jewish/Christian/Muslim or neutral names?

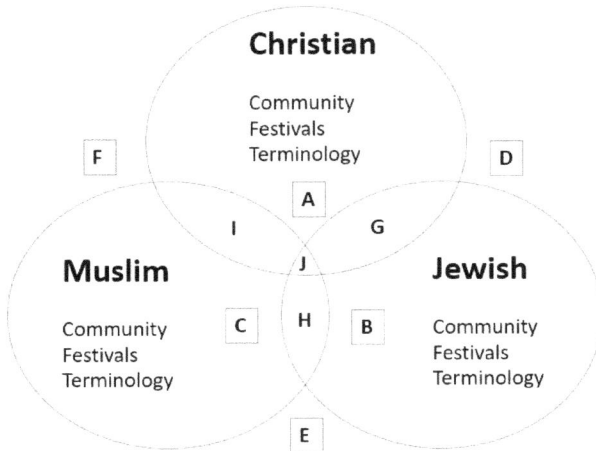

Diagram 2

24. If (religious) communities are tolerant, it is possible to belong to more than one group at the same time (G, H, I or J). From all these options, where do you find yourself?

www.ingramcontent.com/pod-product-compliance
Lightning Source LLC
Chambersburg PA
CBHW071057090426
42737CB00013B/2364